Covering the Courts

A Handbook for Journalists, Second Edition

S. L. Alexander

ROWMAN & LITTLEFIELD PUBLISHERS, INC.
Lanham • Boulder • New York • Oxford

ROWMAN & LITTLEFIELD PUBLISHERS, INC.

Published in the United States of America
by Rowman & Littlefield Publishers, Inc.
A Member of the Rowman & Littlefield Publishing Group
4501 Forbes Boulevard, Suite 200, Lanham, Maryland 20706
www.rowmanlittlefield.com

P. O. Box 317, Oxford OX2 9RU, United Kingdom

British Library Cataloguing in Publication Information Available

Library of Congress Cataloging-in-Publication Data

Alexander, S. L.
    Covering the courts : a handbook for journalists / S.L. Alexander.—
2nd ed.
        p.   cm.
    Includes bibliographical references and index.
    ISBN 0-7425-2021-8 (cloth : alk. paper) — ISBN 0-7425-2022-6 (paper :
alk. paper)
        1. Free press and fair trial—United States.   2. Conduct of court
proceedings—United States.   3. Newspaper court reporting—United
States.   4. Mass media and criminal justice—United States.   5.
Journalism, Legal—United States.   I. Title.
    KF9223.5 .A915   2003
    347.73'12—dc21   2002014812

Printed in the United States of America

♾ ™ The paper used in this publication meets the minimum requirements of American National Standard for Information Sciences—Permanence of Paper for Printed Library Materials, ANSI/NISO Z39.48–1992.

Contents

Figures

Preface

Since the first edition of this handbook was published in 1999, public interest in media coverage of the courts has intensified. High-profile cases include the proceedings surrounding the impeachment of President Bill Clinton; *US v Microsoft*, in which the judge was disqualified from the re-trial for his contact with reporters; the US Supreme Court hearings in the 2000 presidential election case *Bush v Gore*; and coverage of the cases of those involved in the terrorist acts of September 11, 2001.

Some type of camera coverage is now allowed in all fifty states and in many federal courts, and Court TV is now the fastest-growing cable channel, with more than 70 million viewers. Moreover, numerous useful websites have sprung up, a development that has dramatically enhanced the journalist's resources.

The OJ Simpson case retired the title of Trial of the Century. On October 3, 1995, a record-shattering 150 million US viewers watched dramatic coverage of the *California v Simpson* verdict, televised live on three major TV networks as well as three cable TV networks. Coverage of the trial in which Simpson was charged with the murders of his ex-wife Nicole and her friend Ron Goldman was unprecedented: more than 1,000 reporters worked on daily coverage, and more than 2,000 hours of live, gavel-to-gavel coverage aired on cable TV.

As a result, the American public's interest in the judicial process was piqued. However, American Bar Association–Gallup polls showed that coverage of the case resulted in loss of public respect for both lawyers and the media—and lowered confidence in the criminal justice system.

Thus, this much-needed *Handbook* offers support for those concerned with responsible coverage of the courts. It first presents an overview of the judicial system with a discussion of unavoidable fair trial/free press conflicts. A detailed look at criminal procedure helps the journalist gain perspective for accurate coverage of criminal cases, estimated to make up one-half of local news coverage: the parallel examination of civil procedures might encourage more press attention to important matters being litigated.

Since most coverage, however, is of criminal trials, an in-depth description of the process is featured, with separate chapters on pre-trial, trial, and post-trial activity. One chapter deals with coverage of civil cases, another with courtroom cameras for broadcast and netcast. The last chapter includes specific tips from working journalists with a wealth of experience covering courts.

A carefully constructed glossary defines legal terms in language specifically selected for understanding by those trained in journalism rather than law. The appendixes include journalists' codes of ethics, judicial and bar canons and standards, and samples of guidelines for use of cameras in courts.

Thanks again to those who supported the first edition of the *Handbook*; to Loyola University Dean Frank Scully, faculty colleagues, and communications assistants Lynda Favret and Phyllis Aleman for supporting the revision; and to Loyola graphic designers—student Stephen Meyer for the original and instructor Debra Woodfork for the revision.

My appreciation once more to the organizations contributing material for the appendix, and to the dozens of helpful judges, lawyers, court officials and journalists, many of whom are named in chapter 10. The AP's Linda Deutsch; Court TV's Fred Graham, Esq; and Tim O'Brien, Esq; along with Kelli Sager, Esq; Prof. Matthew Bunker, Esq; and Charles Burke, PhD, deserve thanks for reading the original manuscript, as does Dean Lyn Koppel, MA, for reading both editions. Brenda Hadenfeldt, Alden Perkins, and the others at Rowman & Littlefield are also owed a debt of gratitude.

In honor of the good deeds of Director Sandra Chance and the other folk at the University of Florida's Brechner Freedom of Information Center, and my dedication to the family alma mater, I have again assigned them all profits from sales of the *Handbook*.

Finally, my thanks again to my family for their continued support: Dee, Richard, Christopher, Angela, Alexandra—and especially my father and life-long inspiration, Sol Alexander, known around our hometown as "Brother Beans the Lawyer."

Chapter One

Introduction

" 71% OF THE 12,000 JOURNALISTS WHO ARE COVERING THE CASE BELIEVE O.J. HAS TOO MANY LAWYERS."

"Let the jackals in. . . ."
—Judge Lance Ito, presiding judge (referring to the press,
California v Simpson, 1995)

Media coverage of *California v Simpson*[1]—one in a series of high-profile criminal cases described by commentators as "The Trial of the Century"— was indeed pervasive. By the time 150 million television viewers watched coverage of the verdict in October 1995, reporters had spent a year and a half covering the case, and at least thirty books had already been published, with another twenty appearing within the year.[2]

Many people remember the case in which celebrity athlete and media personality OJ Simpson was accused of the murders of his former wife Nicole Brown Simpson and her friend Ron Goldman—from the June 1994 nationally televised "Bronco Chase" down a Los Angeles freeway (which cost the TV networks an estimated seven million dollars in lost ad revenue) through the pre-trial hearings, the nine-month trial, the four-hour jury deliberations, the aforementioned announcement of the verdict, and the hundreds of post-trial media commentaries—not to mention coverage of the subsequent civil case. The press coverage itself was the subject of numerous discussions and critiques.

A description of the coverage of the case by more than 2,000 reporters—representing more than 100 organizations ranging from the *New York Times* to *Dog World*, CBS-TV to *Hard Copy*—along with discussion of the coverage of the subsequent civil case, highlights some of the major issues involved in news coverage of the court system in the US today. Coverage of several subsequent high-profile cases—including the trial of Oklahoma City bomber Timothy McVeigh;[3] the impeachment case of President William (Bill) Clinton;[4] the antitrust case the government brought against Microsoft;[5] the US Supreme Court hearings in the 2000 presidential election case, *Bush v Gore*;[6] and the proceedings involving the September 11 terrorists[7]—further illustrates free press/fair trial issues.

One of the most widely discussed press issues in the Simpson case involved the use of television and still cameras in the courtroom. Presiding Judge Lance Ito held a special hearing in November 1994, at which representatives of the news media such as Kelli Sager convinced him to allow such coverage under the guidelines of the state, typical of those of the forty-nine other states that now also allow some form of camera coverage of courtrooms.

In addition to attaining access from the presiding judge, news organizations must carefully adhere to coverage guidelines or face the threat of loss of the privilege—as happened several times in the Simpson case. For instance, in January 1995, when the regular Court TV camera operator was off work, a substitute accidentally panned the camera too far and showed a brief glimpse of an alternate juror, and Judge Ito threatened to remove the cameras. Again, during closing arguments, when the prosecutor was describing a cut on the defendant's hand, and the camera operator zoomed in to show Simpson writing a note on a legal pad, Judge Ito was angry enough to order the TV cameras to leave the courtroom for an hour before he reconsidered and allowed them to return after imposing a $1,500 fine on the media pool.

Earlier in the trial, Judge Ito had fined an Associated Press (AP) photographer $250 for making a test photo in the courtroom during a break in the proceedings, and he threatened to ban all still photography from the remainder of the trial. Before the trial itself was even underway, the judge had threatened to remove all TV cameras when KNBC-TV had broadcast reports based on erroneous "leaked" information. And at another point, the judge had threatened to "pull the plug" on television coverage if the lawyers did not stop behavior he described as pandering to the cameras.

In the subsequent wrongful-death civil case filed by the families of Nicole Brown Simpson and Ron Goldman,[8] California Superior Court presiding Judge Hiroshi Fujisaki denied a request to allow news cameras in the courtroom, although a pressroom with closed-circuit TV cameras was set up. Coverage of the second trial also was extensive and included nightly re-creations of the day's trial testimony on E! Entertainment Television cable channel.

Camera coverage has also been an issue in the major high-profile trials since *Simpson*. For instance, in the 1997 McVeigh trial, which had been moved to Denver from Oklahoma City,[9] the federal court denied media requests to televise the trial,[10] but the court did allow a first-ever closed-circuit feed so that witnesses, victims, and families could watch from Oklahoma City. At one point, the judge ordered the construction of a barricade in the courtroom so that no members of the jury would be visible in the closed-circuit coverage, but after complaints, members of the press were allowed to change seats so they could see the jurors despite the barricade. Similar restrictions were applied in the subsequent proceedings regarding the trial of Terry Nichols, whose case was separated from McVeigh's.[11]

After McVeigh was convicted, an Internet entertainment network applied to netcast the execution. The court denied the request but did allow a similarly limited closed-circuit feed.[12]

In the Clinton case in 1998, portions of the president's videotaped grand jury testimony were released to broadcasters, and prosecutor Kenneth Starr's report, with recommendations for impeachment, was immediately made available on the Internet. The impeachment hearings themselves were broadcast live.

The appeal court in the government antitrust suit against Microsoft allowed live coverage of oral arguments, while media requests to broadcast federal trial court proceedings in the 2000 presidential election case were denied.[13] Although state rules allowed live broadcasts of the Florida Supreme Court hearings in the election case, the US Supreme Court denied motions to televise the historic hearings but did release coverage to broadcasters fifteen minutes after the conclusion of the session.

Finally, in the case of Zacarias Moussaoui, the first person charged in the September 11 terrorist attacks, the judge denied the request of Court TV to allow broadcast coverage.[14] The Terrorist Victims Courtroom Access Act proposed a limited closed-circuit broadcast similar to that provided the victims in the McVeigh case.[15]

Thus, anyone wishing to improve news coverage of the court system would do well to learn more about cameras in courtrooms. However, the Simpson trial and the subsequent high-profile cases also illustrated other difficulties of courtroom coverage, regardless of the presence or absence of courtroom cameras.

One major issue regarding court coverage is press access to proceedings and to trial participants. Early on in *Simpson*, Judge Ito proposed a blanket "gag order," restraining trial participants from talking with the press. (California was one of the states that had not adopted specific American Bar Association [ABA] rules describing permissible conduct for lawyers during a trial.) After a hearing with representatives of eight news organizations and the American Civil Liberties Union (ACLU), the judge withdrew his proposed restriction. A gag order imposed throughout the subsequent civil trial was also modified after media challenges.

However, the media were not successful in attempts to lift a gag in the McVeigh case,[16] and in the Clinton case, witness Monica Lewinsky was bound by a gag order under terms of an immunity agreement with prosecutor Ken Starr.

Access to evidence and proceedings is another issue of concern to the courtroom reporter. Early in the Simpson case, journalists successfully employed the *California Public Records Act* to obtain copies of 911 tapes of calls Nicole Simpson had made during earlier domestic disturbances involving the defendant. The tapes were released just in time for the local 5 P.M. TV newscasts and received wide coverage, which led to defense charges the prosecution was attempting to manipulate public opinion before a jury had been selected.

Later, the judge denied media permission to copy at least three of the most gruesome photographs of the murder victims; he speculated that the media would use them in an inappropriate and sensationalistic manner.

The media were also unsuccessful in attempts to obtain access to sealed documents in the McVeigh case,[17] although some documents were eventually unsealed in *Clinton v Jones*,[18] the sexual harassment case that was related to the Clinton impeachment.

In *US v Microsoft*, a federal appeals panel ordered access to records and proceedings, including twenty-four hours of videotaped depositions of CEO Bill Gates.[19] However, most records and hearings remained closed during pretrial proceedings of accused terrorists throughout much of the year following the September 11 attacks.[20]

Another issue that journalists must learn to deal with is confidentiality of sources. During jury selection in *Simpson*, the defense had moved to subpoena two representatives of KNBC-TV—reporter Tracie Savage and General Manager Carole Black, along with the Los Angeles police chief and his spokesman—in an attempt to discover the source of leaked information. The judge, however, refused to hold a hearing on the matter at that time.

In August of 1995, subpoenas were issued again, this time for Savage and for magazine and book author Joseph Bosco. They were to be asked to reveal their sources for stories they had done about blood tests made on Simpson's socks: according to the prosecutor, both had reported information on the tests before the tests had been conducted. And their stories had an impact on the case: the defense suggested the presumed police source of the leak must have been involved in some sort of conspiracy to frame Simpson. Judge Ito ultimately decided both reporters were covered by California's shield law and did not have to reveal their sources, but any journalist relying on confidential sources during the course of courtroom coverage needs to be aware of the possibility of a contempt citation, with a possible fine or even jail sentence for interfering with a defendant's due process rights.

In fact, journalists need to understand that a presiding judge charged with maintaining a decorous courtroom has great power to find anyone in the courtroom in contempt of court. For example, during jury selection in the Simpson case, Judge Ito temporarily revoked the permanent seat pass of the *Los Angeles Daily News* as punishment for a leaked story detailing a jury questionnaire (although he backed down after a legal challenge). During this same pre-trial period, the judge took the unusual step of canceling a session of jury selection while he consulted with other judges about the propriety of his request to three different news organizations for them to delay planned interviews with Faye Resnick, author of a lurid book that claimed Simpson had stalked his ex-wife and threatened to kill her. Larry King of CNN (which had sent some seventy people to cover the trial) complied with the judge's request; however, both CBS-TV and syndicated talk-show host Maury Povich went ahead with the interviews as scheduled. Journalists must know their rights regarding such requests from a presiding judge.

The court's power to find journalists in contempt is broad. For instance, Judge Ito removed from the trial both a reporter from Court TV and one from *USA Today* for whispering too loudly during the proceedings. The judge controlled a hidden security camera during the trial that he used to catch courtroom miscreants: he reprimanded a KCAL-TV reporter for chewing gum in a distracting manner and publicly showed her on tape as an object lesson to others.

A notable example of press impact on the judicial process in *Simpson* involved "checkbook journalism"—payment by news organizations to potential witnesses to tell their stories prior to testifying in court. Several witnesses were never called to testify because their testimony was considered tainted. These included the cutlery-store owner who claimed he had recently sold Simpson a knife (and was reportedly paid $12,500 for his story by the *National Enquirer*). Simpson's neighbor Jill Shively never was called: she reportedly had been paid $2,600 by the *Star* and $5,000 by *Hard Copy* to describe her claim she had seen the defendant frantically driving around neighborhood streets at the time of the murders.

The ex-wife of witness Brian "Kato" Kaelin appeared on *Inside Edition*, where her story contradicted some of Kaelin's sworn testimony. Kaelin himself had been offered a quarter of a million dollars by the *National Enquirer* for his story. And the managing editor of the *Enquirer* appeared on CNN with Larry King and offered Simpson's associate AC Cowlings one million dollars for his version of events.

The practice of paying prospective witnesses during the Simpson trial, added to similar problems during other high-profile trials such as those of Eric and Lyle Menendez,[21] led to quick passage of a special law in California making it a crime for prospective witnesses to accept money from reporters. The law was successfully challenged on constitutional grounds in federal court. A similar state law forbidding jurors from accepting more than $50 for their stories prior to ninety days after the end of the trial was also passed— and it too was successfully challenged. However, in spite of this and the fact that most of the problems in this area were caused by "tabloid" journalists, many courtroom participants fail to make any distinctions and remain wary of all journalists due to concern with possible interference with due process.

Although most members of the establishment press presumably attempted accurate and fair coverage of the Simpson case, some serious errors were made. For instance, within days of the murder, the *Los Angeles Daily News* incorrectly reported that an "entrenching tool" believed to be the murder weapon had been recovered by the police, and although this story received wide coverage, no such weapon had been found—or even sought. Nor, despite news reports, had a bloody ski mask been discovered, nor were there bloody clothes in Simpson's washer nor bloodstains on his golf bag. In a more serious error, a reporter for KCBS-TV reported that prosecutor Marcia Clark had visited the defendant's estate before obtaining a proper warrant, another false story that received wide coverage. In this case, the reporter had to apologize on-air for his error.

To be fair, in most instances of coverage of *Simpson*, it appeared even tabloid newspapers, particularly the *National Enquirer*—which at times had twenty reporters out on the story—did attempt accuracy. The *New York Times* published at least two articles praising the *Enquirer*'s coverage, and during the trial ABC-TV's *Nightline* program aired a story on the paper's coverage complete with a visit to the newspaper's headquarters in Florida.

But with thousands of journalists and media personnel spending so much time covering the case out in Camp OJ, the general impression of the coverage of the case was of a media circus. Of course, the trial included more than 100 witnesses and nearly 1,000 pieces of evidence and cost the taxpayers of Los Angeles about nine million dollars. But the media added to the circus atmosphere: at the least, some members of the media harassed the principals in the case; interfered with the witnesses; disclosed information prematurely; or, in the worst cases, published incorrect speculation. The judge supervising the grand jury investigation early in the Simpson case had blamed the publicity for the apparently unprecedented decision to abruptly halt the secret grand jury and move right to a preliminary hearing in the case.

The McVeigh case also involved publicity concerns. Before trial, Timothy McVeigh unsuccessfully moved to have the case dismissed on grounds he could never obtain a fair trial due to massive prejudicial publicity.[22] After trial, he unsuccessfully appealed the conviction on grounds including the publication of reports of a confession on Internet websites, including that of the *Dallas Morning News*.[23]

In all fairness, some of the blame for the chaotic atmosphere surrounding such high-profile cases as *Simpson* rested with the members of the legal profession themselves. Several of the lawyers involved were rightfully accused of trying the case in the media with their frequent press conferences, press releases, and interviews with reporters. Even Judge Ito was criticized for participating in a five-part TV interview prior to the trial, as well as for granting requests to other judges, writers, and celebrity reporters to sit in on portions of the case and to visit with him in his chambers.

In the Microsoft case, the appeal court disqualified the trial judge, Thomas Penfield Jackson, from hearing the re-trial because Jackson had talked to reporters during the months between the end of the presentation of the case and the issuing of his verdict: presumably he had been hoping a court-ordered negotiator would be able to reach a settlement in the case. The appeal court said the judge's actions in "giving secret interviews to select reporters" presented an "appearance of partiality."[24]

Although the responsibility for a fair trial remains with the presiding judge, members of the news media must make every effort to avoid interference with due process.

Thus, as is clear from the coverage of not only the exceptional Simpson cases but other recent high-profile trials mentioned above, the typical journalist needs to understand better the process of judicial administration in the US (discussed here in chapter 2), including criminal and civil procedures (chapters 3 and 4).

Next, the journalist needs to learn the best methods of pre-trial preparation, such as the means of access to judicial records and the importance of hearings and plea bargains (chapter 5). Regarding the trial itself, he must understand both his rights—such as what to do if a judge attempts to close a trial—as well as his responsibilities (chapter 6). The journalist should learn the best methods of covering the post-trial phase, including the appellate process (chapter 7), and how the entire process differs when a case is followed through the civil court system (chapter 8).

The journalist—particularly the news photographer and the broadcast journalist—needs to be familiar with the guidelines for use of cameras in court (chapter 9).

Finally—and perhaps most importantly—the journalist would benefit from the experiences of other working journalists. Offered here (in chapter 10) are specific tips for coverage as well as suggestions for topics appropriate for enterprise stories—those initiated by the reporter or editor and generally ignored in favor of simply covering court cases—in order to provide the public with a more complete understanding of the process of judicial administration.

NOTES

1. *In re California v Simpson*, No BAO 97211 (Proceedings 11/17/94).

2. In addition to the books written by trial participants, as well as daily news coverage in print and broadcast media from 13 June 1994 through February 1997, see, generally, the following: S. L. Alexander, "The Impact of *California v Simpson* on Cameras in the Courtroom," *Judicature* 79:4 (January–February 1996): 169–172; Don DeBenedictus, "The National Verdict," *ABA Journal* (October 1994): 52–55; Lincoln Caplan, "The Failure (and Promise) of Legal Journalism," in *Postmortem,* ed. Jeffrey Abramson (New York: Basic Books, 1996), 199–207; Steve Keeva, "Storm Warnings," *ABA Journal* (June 1995): 77–78; Daniel Petrocelli, *Triumph of Justice* (New York: Crown Publishers, 1998); Kelli Sager, "First Amendment Issues in the OJ Simpson Trial," *Communications Lawyer* (Winter 1995): 3–7; Jacqueline Sharkey, "Judgment Calls," *American Journalism Review* (September 1994): 18–27; and Paul Thaler, *The Spectacle* (Westport, Conn.: Praeger, 1997).

3. *US v McVeigh & Nichols*, 169 F 3d 1255 (US 10th Cir Ct), 1997.

4. *US v Clinton*, US GPO S doc 106th Cong 1st Sess, 1999, Sen 106–104.

5. *US v Microsoft*, US Dist Ct DC 98–1232, 98–1233, 2000.

6. *Bush v Gore*, 531 US 98, 2000.

7. *US v Moussaoui*, US Dist Ct ED Va, No 01–455-A, 2002.

8. *In re Rufo v Simpson*, Ca Sup Ct No SC 031947 (23 August 1996).

9. *US v McVeigh and Nichols*, 918 F Supp 1467 (US Dist Ct, WD OK), 1996.

10. *US v McVeigh and Nichols*, 931 F Supp 753 (US Dist Ct, Dist CO), 1996.

11. *Nichols v Dist Ct Oklahoma Cty*, 2000 OK CR 12, PR-2000–703 (10th OK Ct Crim Appl), 2000.

12. *Entertain v Lappin*, 134 F Supp 2d 1002 (US Dist Ct, SD Ind), 2001.

13. *In re Siegel v LePore*, 29 Med L Rptr 1190 (US Dist Ct, SD Fla), 2000.

14. *US v Moussaoui*, see note 7.

15. The Terrorist Victims Courtroom Access Act, 107th Cong, 2nd Sess, 2002 S 1858, 107S 1858, 2001.

16. *US v McVeigh in re Petition of Colorado-Oklahoma Media* 964 F Supp 313 (US Dist Ct, Dist CO), 1997.

17. *US v McVeigh*, 119 F 3d 806 (US 10 Cir Ct Appl), 1997.

18. *Jones v Clinton*, US Dist Ct ED Ark, No LR-C-94-290, 27 Med L Rptr 1156, 1998.

19. *US v Microsoft*, 334 US App DC 165, 1999.

20. "Feds Release Transcript of Immigration Hearings," RCFP *The News Media and the Law* (Spring 2002): 47.

21. *California v Menendez*, Supr Ct LA Cty, SA 002727, SA 002728, 1994; Ca Supr Ct SC 031947, 1995.

22. *US v McVeigh*, 955 F Supp 1281 (US Dist Ct, Dist CO), 1997.

23. *US v McVeigh*, 153 F 3d 1166 (US 10th Cir Ct Appl), 1998.

24. *US v Microsoft*, 253 F 3d 34, 2001, "Judicial Misconduct" at 106–118.

Chapter Two

The Judicial System

"*Lights! Camera! Justice!*"

The conflict between the First Amendment rights of a free press and the Sixth Amendment rights to a fair trial (or, as the legal community sees it, the conflict between fair trial and free press) has been present at least since the controversy over coverage of the 1807 treason trial of Aaron Burr.[1] Although a recent approach advanced by scholars such as Matthew Bunker suggests the First Amendment should require balancing tests be set aside in favor of set rules allowing access to all aspects of the criminal justice system, this idea has met with little support.[2] Thus, decisions in US Supreme Court cases highlight issues such as prejudicial publicity, access to courts and court records, "gag orders," and use of courtroom cameras as the courts continue to balance First Amendment and Sixth Amendment concerns.

FREE PRESS/FAIR TRIAL

The 1966 decision in *Sheppard v Maxwell*[3] dealt with pre-trial publicity. Dr. Sam Sheppard had been tried for the murder of his wife in 1954. A five-hour, three-day inquest had been televised "live"; a prisoner's claim she had borne Sheppard's child was widely publicized; and during the trial a debate on the case was broadcast live. The US Supreme Court held 8–1 that due process had been denied, and the conviction was overturned.

Often overlooked in the discussion of the case is the Court's holding that the blame lay less with the press than with the trial judge for failing to take proper precautions to assure a fair trial. In fact, Justice Tom Clark, speaking for the Court, said, "A responsible press has always been regarded as the handmaiden of effective judicial administration, especially in the criminal field." He added that the press "guards against the miscarriage of justice by subjecting the police, prosecutors, and judicial processes to extensive public scrutiny and criticism."[4]

The Court in *Sheppard* suggested the trial judge could have taken several steps to lessen the impact of pre-trial publicity. For instance, the judge could have ordered a delay in the start of the trial to allow the publicity to die down. (Other alternatives are discussed in detail in chapter 3.)

The US Supreme Court has also ruled in several other cases involving the effects of prejudicial publicity. For instance, in *Rideau v Louisiana* (1963),[5] the Court overturned the conviction of a murderer whose televised confession had been seen by the thousands of potential jurors who lived near the trial site. Similarly, the conviction in another murder case, *Irvin v Dowd* (1961),[6] was overturned due to—among other grounds—news reports of Irvin's earlier criminal convictions.

However, in 1991, the High Court ruled that individual prospective jurors do not have to be asked specifically what news coverage they have read or heard or watched about the case during jury selection. In *Mu'Min v Virginia*,[7] the Court held that as long as the judge has questioned jurors in general about their ability to put aside any information based on pretrial publicity and decide a case solely on the evidence in the courtroom, there may be no cause for overturning a conviction despite extensive publicity.

Another major relevant free press–fair trial issue involves restrictive orders against publicizing a case, such as the prior restraints dealt with in *Nebraska Press Association v Stuart*.[8] In this 1976 case, before the opening of a murder trial in which a Nebraska farmhand was to be tried for the brutal murders of all six members of a family (for which the defendant was ultimately convicted), the judge ordered news media to refrain from publishing any confessions or other material "strongly implicative" of the guilt of the suspect.[9]

Speaking for a unanimous Court, Chief Justice Warren Burger held that the trial judge should have considered alternative means of protecting the defendant's rights, such as a change of venue or a continuance, rather than restraints on the press. According to Burger, "[P]rior restraints on speech and publication are the most serious and the least tolerable infringement on First Amendment rights."[10]

Then in *US v Noriega*,[11] a drug case against the former leader of Panama, CNN broadcast tapes of conversations of the imprisoned Manuel Noriega but balked at turning the tapes over to the trial judge to determine whether broadcasting the tapes—just prior to a restraining order—violated Noriega's Sixth Amendment rights. CNN was found in contempt for its actions, although the judge eventually found the tapes had posed no threat to Noriega's rights. The US Supreme Court let stand the contempt citation against CNN.

And as the 1997 Oklahoma City bomber case and other later cases demonstrated, despite *Nebraska*, some restraints (to be discussed in chapter 6) may be upheld under certain circumstances.

A third area in which the Court has balanced First Amendment and Sixth Amendment rights regards access to courts: here, too, the Court generally tips the scale in favor of free expression. The Court held in 1946 in *Craig v Harney:* "[A] trial is a public event. What transpires in the courtroom is public property. . . . Those who see and hear what transpired can report it with impunity."[12]

However, in 1979's *Gannett v DePasquale*[13] the Court held the press had no constitutional right to attend pre-trial hearings; the guarantee of a public trial was for the benefit of the accused, not the public. But in later cases such as *Press-Enterprise v Riverside Sup. Ct. I*[14] and *II*,[15] and *El Vocero v Puerto Rico*,[16] the Court held defendants must show that openness of pre-trial activity would cause "substantial probability" of danger to a fair trial.

And in the 1980 landmark *Richmond Newspapers v Virginia*,[17] the Court held a defendant's request to exclude the press from his murder trial should not have been granted. Chief Justice Burger described the history of open trials: "People in an open society do not demand infallibility from their institutions, but it is difficult for them to accept what they are prohibited from observing."[18] He concluded: "Plainly it would be difficult to single out any aspect of government of higher concern and importance to the people than the manner in which criminal trials are conducted."[19]

Richmond notwithstanding, the press is not guaranteed access to all aspects of the judicial process. For instance, the US Supreme Court has yet to rule definitively on a specific right of access to noncriminal proceedings.[20] However, lower courts have held that civil cases are generally presumed to be public (see chapter 8).

And the High Court has not yet considered the propriety of use of anonymous jurors, a growing problem from the journalistic point of view (see chapter 6 for lower court cases).

Nor has the High Court ruled on the right, prior to trial, of access to evidence gathered from interviewing potential witnesses or from documents. The trend in lower courts seems to be generally to deny press access in this area, although courts have supported the right of access to material actually used as evidence in court, including the right of broadcast journalists to copy tapes used as evidence (for example, in the FBI bribery sting targeting public officials, the NBC "Abscam" case in 1981).[21] The right is not absolute, as demonstrated by the follow-up to the Watergate coverage, in *Nixon v Warner Communications*, decided in 1978[22] (see chapter 6 for lower court cases).

The High Court has generally supported the press in several other areas. For instance, the Court limited the power of judges to punish the press for publishing confidential material in *Landmark Communications v Virginia*, a case involving a judicial investigation;[23] in *Smith v Daily Mail*, a case involving publication of names of juvenile defendants for a non-sex offense;[24] and in *Globe Newspaper v Superior Court*,[25] a sex-offense case. Two landmark privacy cases (*Cox Broadcasting v Cohn*[26] and *Florida Star v BJF*[27]) held the press is not liable for invasion of privacy for reporting information that is part of the court record or lawfully obtained from public officials.

The journalist should also be aware of the requirement supported by a lower court (in *US v Dickinson*)[28] that members of the press must follow a judge's orders even if they are later determined to be unconstitutional (although a different lower court, in *In re Providence Journal*,[29] has held that if a publisher makes a "good faith effort" to appeal a "transparently unconstitutional" order and was denied a hearing, he might go ahead and publish in the interim).

Journalists who fail to obey a judge's order will be found in contempt of court and may be punished by a fine or even a jail term. One area of contention involves demands that reporters turn over names of sources for stories or unpublished notes or videotape. In *Branzburg v Hayes*,[30] the Supreme Court ruled that the First Amendment does not protect journalists in all circumstances, and particularly when a reporter witnesses criminal acts and is ordered to appear before a grand jury, it is likely he will be forced to comply to avoid a finding of contempt.

However, in the area of courtroom cameras the law is most unsettled when the High Court weighs First Amendment versus Sixth Amendment rights. Even such a First Amendment absolutist as the late Justice William Douglas called cameras an insidious intrusion into the decorum of the court and the judicial process.

CAMERAS IN COURTS

Although Canon 35, the American Bar Association's 1937 prohibition against courtroom cameras, stood virtually intact for nearly fifty years, revisionists have brought one or two curious aspects of the ban to light. For instance, it had been generally accepted that the behavior of cameramen inside the courtroom at the New Jersey trial of Bruno Hauptmann for the kidnapping and murder of Charles Lindbergh's baby[31]—a trial that newsman H. L. Mencken called "the greatest story since the Resurrection"[32]—inspired the ABA to pass the ban. However, critics such as Richard Kielbowicz and Susanna Barber have pointed out other factors that contributed to the circus-like atmosphere of the Hauptmann trial, and they maintain that the ban should not be viewed solely as the result of courtroom cameras as employed in the 1935 trial.[33]

Furthermore, participants in the trial have also defended the 120 cameramen who (along with 700 newsmen) covered the trial. Photographer Joseph Costa of the old *New York Morning World* covered the trial and said although some still photographs and film had been taken surreptitiously—in violation of the judge's order to keep cameras off during the actual proceedings—the idea that it was cameramen, particularly the four photographers and one newsreel cameraman who ran the pool inside the courtroom, who disrupted the Hauptmann trial was myth.[34] And *Hauptmann* juror Ethel Stockton insisted none of the photographers caused a problem. She said, "I didn't even know they had cameras there until I got home after the trial and saw the pictures in the newspaper."[35]

Although the factors that led to the ban are better understood today than they once were, the fact remains that in 1937 the ABA passed a total ban on courtroom cameras: Canon 35, Improper Publicizing of Court Proceedings.[36]

Canon 35 remained in effect for nearly fifty years. There was only one significant revision: television was specifically added to the prohibition in 1952. Although there was continued debate about revising or even revoking Canon 35, and some camera coverage was permitted in a handful of state courts, by 1965 states everywhere except Colorado and Texas had adopted bans on courtroom cameras.[37]

In 1965, *Estes v Texas*[38] became the first landmark courtroom camera case. In *Estes*, the High Court overturned the swindling conviction of Billie Sol Estes based on denial of due process. A pre-trial hearing had been carried live on television and radio, and although live broadcasting was forbidden during the trial itself, silent cameras operated intermittently and excerpts were shown on news programs each night.

Justice Tom Clark, writing for a plurality, held television might improperly influence jurors, impair the testimony of witnesses, distract judges, and burden defendants. However, Justice Potter Stewart dissented, saying, "The idea of imposing upon any medium of communication the burden of justifying its presence is contrary to where I had always thought the presumption must lie in the area of First Amendment freedoms."[39]

After *Estes* and *Sheppard*, the ABA strengthened its position on Canon 35, and when in 1972 the organization revised its Code, Canon 35—now allowing cameras for educational uses only—was renamed Canon 3A(7). Finally, after the *Chandler* decision (discussed below) and the increased use of courtroom cameras in the states, at the 1982 ABA convention the delegates voted to revise Canon 3A(7) to allow for news camera coverage at the discretion of each state's high court:

> A judge should prohibit broadcasting, televising, recording, or photographing in courtrooms and areas immediately adjacent thereto during sessions of court, or recesses between sessions, except that under rules prescribed by supervising appellate court or other appropriate authority, a judge may authorize broadcasting, televising, recording and photographing of judicial proceedings in the courtrooms and areas immediately adjacent thereto consistent with the right of the parties to a fair trial and subject to express conditions, limitations, and guidelines which allow such coverage in a manner that will be unobtrusive, will not distract the trial participants, and will not otherwise interfere with the administration of justice.[40]

In the second US Supreme Court landmark camera case, 1981's *Chandler v Florida*,[41] two Miami Beach policemen appealed their burglary convictions on the grounds the cameras (in the courtroom during Florida's experiment) had denied them due process. Chief Justice Warren Burger delivered the 8–0 opinion of the court, which upheld the convictions and said the mere presence of cameras did not violate fair trial rights. Justice Burger concluded that although "[D]angers lurk in this as in most experiments," unless television coverage under all conditions were prohibited by the Constitution, states must be free to experiment.[42]

As Florida and other states have continued to experiment with courtroom cameras, two modest trends among reported cases might be noted. The first is toward more generally allowing cameras into the courts absent exceptional circumstances. Moreover, most criminal convictions are upheld despite some defendants' claims of denial of due process because of the presence of courtroom camera coverage. In fact, with one or two minor exceptions, it appears no convictions in either state or federal courts have been overturned due to courtroom cameras since the likewise failed attempt in *Chandler*. And state courts seem to be reluctant to uphold citations for contempt when judges seek to punish broadcast journalists and news photographers who violate bans against camera coverage.

As mentioned earlier, as of 2002, all fifty states permit some type of camera coverage, whether on an experimental or permanent basis (See Figure 2.1: Cameras in State Courts). However, the goal of the journalist, regardless of the presence or absence of cameras, is to present accurate coverage with a minimum of disruption to the unique process of judicial administration under the US Constitution—the process described in chapters 3 and 4.

Figure 2.1

Cameras in State Courts

States with Permanent Rules

State	Level	Division
Alabama	Trial & Appellate	Civil & Criminal
Alaska	Trial & Appellate	Civil & Criminal
Arizona	Trial & Appellate	Civil & Criminal
Arkansas	Trial & Appellate	Civil & Criminal
California	Trial & Appellate	Civil & Criminal
Colorado	Trial & Appellate	Civil & Criminal
Connecticut	Trial & Appellate	Civil & Criminal
Florida	Trial & Appellate	Civil & Criminal
Georgia	Trial & Appellate	Civil & Criminal
Hawaii	Trial & Appellate	Civil & Criminal
Idaho	Supreme Court in Boise; Supreme Court on circuit	
Illinois	Appellate	
Iowa	Trial & Appellate	Civil & Criminal
Kansas	Trial & Appellate	Civil & Criminal
Kentucky	Trial & Appellate	Civil & Criminal
Louisiana	Appellate	
Maine	Trial	Civil
Maryland	Trial & Appellate	Civil
Massachusetts	Trial & Appellate	
Michigan	Trial & Appellate	Civil & Criminal
Minnesota	Appellate	
Mississippi	Supreme Court	Civil & Criminal
Missouri	Trial & Appellate	Civil & Criminal
Montana	Trial & Appellate	Civil & Criminal
Nebraska	Appellate	
Nevada	Trial & Appellate	Civil & Criminal
New Hampshire	Trial & Appellate	Civil & Criminal
New Jersey	Trial & Appellate	
New Mexico	Trial & Appellate	Civil & Criminal
New York	Appellate	
North Carolina	Trial & Appellate	Civil & Criminal
North Dakota	Trial & Supreme Court	Civil & Criminal
Ohio	Trial & Appellate	Civil & Criminal
Oklahoma	Trial & Appellate	Civil & Criminal
Oregon	Trial	Civil & Criminal
Rhode Island	Trial & Appellate	Civil & Criminal
South Carolina	Trial & Appellate	Civil & Criminal
South Dakota	Supreme Court	
Tennessee	Trial & Appellate	Civil & Criminal
Texas	Trial & Appellate	Civil & Criminal
Utah	Supreme Court	
Vermont	Trial & Appellate	Civil & Criminal
Virginia	Trial & Appellate	Civil & Criminal
Washington	Trial & Appellate	Civil & Criminal
West Virginia	Trial & Appellate	Civil & Criminal
Wisconsin	Trial & Appellate	Civil & Criminal
Wyoming	Trial & Appellate	Civil & Criminal

Figure 2.1 (Continued)

Cameras in State Courts

States with Experimental Rules

State	Level	Division
Delaware	Supreme Court	Civil
Idaho	Court of Appeals Trial Courts	Civil & Criminal
Indiana	Appellate Courts	
Minnesota	Trial Courts	Civil & Criminal
New Jersey	Municipal Courts	Civil & Criminal
Pennsylvania	Trial, non-jury	Civil, Superior Court

Summary of State Rules

States with Permanent Rules*

Approved for Trial and Appellate Courts	36
Approved for Trial Courts Only	2
Approved for Appellate Courts Only	8

States with Experimental Rules*

Approved for Trial and Appellate Courts	1
Approved for Trial Courts Only	4
Approved for Appellate Courts Only	2

Total states allowing cameras in a courtroom	50
Total states allowing cameras in a criminal trial	37

*Note: Some states fall into more than one category.

{Courtesy National Center for State Courts, Knowledge and Information Services, Williamsburg, VA 23187, 2002. Reprinted with permission. There are additional restrictions on camera usage in individual states. See *Figure 9, Courtroom Camera Guidelines,* Radio-TV News Directors Association.}

NOTES

1. *US v Burr*, 25 Fed Cas 49 No 14692g (1807). See, generally, Douglas Campbell, *Free Press v Fair Trial* (Westport, Conn.: Praeger, 1994); Alfredo Garcia, "Clash of the Titans," *Santa Clara Law Review* 32 (1992): 1107–1133; Randall Kennedy, "Cast a Cautious Eye on the Supreme Court," *Media Studies Journal* 12:1 (Winter 1998): 112–123; and Bernard Schwartz, *Decision* (New York: Oxford University Press, 1996). Also, "Federal Rules of Civil Procedure," "Federal Rules of Criminal Procedure," and "Federal Rules of Evidence for Judges and Magistrates," *Black's Law Dictionary*, 6th ed. (St. Paul, Minn.: West Publishing, 1990); and Yale Kamisar et al., *Modern Criminal Procedure*, 6th ed. (St. Paul, Minn.: West Publishing, 1986).

2. Matthew Bunker, *Justice and the Media* (Mahwah, N.J.: Lawrence Erlbaum, 1997).

3. *Sheppard v Maxwell, Warden*, 384 US 333 (1966).

4. *Sheppard v Maxwell*, 350.

5. *Rideau v Louisiana*, 373 US 723 (1963). (In 2001, the US Supreme Court let stand a lower court decision overturning Rideau's conviction on grounds of exclusion of blacks from the grand jury. He was immediately re-indicted and as of 2002 scheduled for re-trial.)

6. *Irvin v Dowd*, 366 US 717 (1961).

7. *Mu'Min v Virginia*, 501 US 1269 (1991).

8. *Nebraska Press Association v Stuart*, 427 US 539 (1976).

9. *Nebraska Press Association v Stuart*, 544.

10. *Nebraska Press Association v Stuart*, 559.

11. *US v Noriega*, 752 F Supp 1032 (US Dist Ct DC) 1990; *CNN v Noriega and US*, 917 F 2d 1543 (US 12th Cir Ct Appl), 1990; *cert den* 498 US 976 (1990).

12. *Craig v Harney*, 331 US 367, 374 (1947).

13. *Gannett v DePasquale*, 443 US 368 (1979).

14. *Press Enterprise v Riverside Sup Ct I*, 464 US 501 (1984). See also *Waller v Georgia*, 467 US 39 (1984).

15. *Press Enterprise v Riverside Sup Ct II*, 478 US 1 (1986).

16. *El Vocero de Puerto Rico v Puerto Rico*, 508 US 147 (1993).

17. *Richmond Newspapers v Virginia*, 488 US 555 (1980).

18. *Richmond Newspapers v Virginia*, 572.

19. *Richmond Newspapers v Virginia*, 575.

20. See, for example, *Seattle Times v Rhinehart*, 467 US 20 (1984).

21. *In re NBC*, 648 F2d 814 (US 3rd Cir Ct Appl), 1981.

22. *Nixon v Warner Communications*, 435 US 589 (1978).

23. *Landmark Communications v Virginia*, 435 US 829 (1978).

24. *Smith v Daily Mail*, 443 US 97 (1979).

25. *Globe Newspaper v Sup Ct*, 457 US 596 (1982).

26. *Cox Broadcasting v Cohn*, 420 US 469 (1975).

27. *Florida Star v BJF*, 491 US 524 (1989).

28. *US v Dickinson*, 465 F2d 496 (US 5th Cir Ct Appl), 1972.

29. *In re Providence Journal*, 820 F2d 1342 (US 1st Cir Ct Appl), 1986.

30. *Branzburg v Hayes*, 408 US 665 (1972).

31. *New Jersey v Hauptmann*, 180 A 809 (NJ Sup Ct), 1935.

32. H. L. Mencken, cited by Lloyd Chiasson in *The Press on Trial* (Westport, Conn.: Greenwood Press, 1997), 17.

33. See, for example, Richard Kielbowicz, "The Story Behind the Adoption of the Ban on Courtroom Cameras," *Judicature* 63:1 (June–July 1979): 14–23; Susanna Barber, *News Cameras in the Courtroom* (Norwood, N.J.: Ablex Publishing Corp., 1987); and S. L. Alexander, "Curious History," *Mass Comm Review* 18:3 (1991): 31–37ff.

34. Joseph Costa, "Cameras in Courtrooms"(manuscript, Ball State University, 1980).

35. Ethel Stockton, interview by author, Ocala, Florida, 31 July 1989.

36. Canon 35, *ABA Reports* 62 (1937): 1134–1135.

37. Frank White, "Cameras in the Courtroom," *Journalism Monographs* 60 (April 1979).

38. *Estes v Texas*, 381 US 532 (1965).

39. *Estes v Texas,* 615.

40. Canon 3A(7), *Lawyers Manual on Professional Conduct* (Chicago: ABA, 1982).

41. *Chandler v Florida*, 449 US 560 (1981).

42. *Chandler v Florida,* 582.

Chapter Three

Criminal Procedure

The judicial system in the US is an **adversarial system**, that is, it pits one side against another, generally with a judge and jury as mediators. The legal process must be carried out in accord with **due process**—procedural safeguards called for in the US Constitution.

In **civil actions**, which seek to resolve conflict between people or institutions, both **litigants**—the **plaintiff**, who brings the charges, and the party often referred to as the **respondent**, who is being sued—may represent the government, private individuals, groups, or corporations in conflict. In **criminal actions**, which seek to enforce codes of behavior, the government is always the plaintiff, charging the **defendant** with breaking the laws of society.

Misdemeanors are minor crimes—such as theft of something of low property value, drunk and disorderly conduct, or prostitution—for which the penalty may be a fine or a short jail term. **Felonies** are major crimes—ranging from arson, larceny, and burglary to assault, rape, and murder—for which the penalty may be a sentence of a year or longer in the state prison or even the death penalty (with such cases referred to as **capital crimes**).

In keeping with the federal type of government in the US (i.e., fifty state governments and one national government), the court system is a dual system. The state courts and the federal courts are each divided into three levels: a **court of original jurisdiction** (or **trial** court), where the case begins; an intermediate court (or **appellate court**), which may **review** or re-examine the findings of a lower court; and a **court of final resolution** (or high court), generally referred to as a **supreme court**, with the ultimate power of review over all lower courts in its jurisdiction.

On the state level, each state designs its own court system. Generally a state's lowest courts may be assigned geographically by city or county into local courts such as general courts and special courts—traffic courts, small claims courts, juvenile courts, probate courts, and family courts. Very often the state's lowest level courts, such as justice of the peace courts, do not keep transcripts of proceedings; only when such a written **record** is available may a case be appealed. In about half the states, at the intermediate level, courts may be divided into appellate districts, often grouping several counties together. The state supreme courts are generally located in the state capitals. (See Figure 3.1: The State Court System.)

On the federal level, the country is divided into ninety-four trial courts, called **district courts**, with each state assigned from one to four federal district courts. If the decision of a trial court is appealed, the case may move to one of the thirteen federal appellate courts, called **circuit courts**, and if the decision of the appeal court is unsatisfactory, the option may remain of appealing some cases to the US Supreme Court (also called the High Court). Also, in some state cases involving constitutional issues, appeals may end up in the US Supreme Court. As a court of limited jurisdiction, the Supreme Court generally may hear only actual disputes, not hypothetical questions or those that already have been resolved and are thus **moot**. (See Figure 3.2: The Federal Court System.)

THE PRE-TRIAL PROCESS

A minor case may enter the criminal justice system as the result of a **citation**—for instance, a police officer may issue a traffic ticket. A more serious

Figure 3.1

The State Court System

SUPREME COURT OF LOUISIANA

| Court of Appeal First Circuit *Baton Rouge* | Court of Appeal Second Circuit *Shreveport* | Court of Appeal Third Circuit *Lake Charles* | Court of Appeal Fourth Circuit *New Orleans* | Court of Appeal Fifth Circuit *Gretna* |

Court of Appeal First Circuit — *Baton Rouge*
- District Courts 16 Parishes
- Family Court / Juvenile Court *East Baton Rouge*
- 13 City Courts
- 1 Parish Court

Court of Appeal Second Circuit — *Shreveport*
- District Courts 20 Parishes
- Juvenile Court *Caddo Parish*
- 10 City Courts

Court of Appeal Third Circuit — *Lake Charles*
- District Courts 21 Parishes
- 22 City Courts

Court of Appeal Fourth Circuit — *New Orleans*
- District Courts 3 Parishes
- Juvenile Court *Orleans Parish*
- 4 City Courts

Court of Appeal Fifth Circuit — *Gretna*
- District Courts 4 Parishes
- Juvenile Court *Jefferson Parish*
- 2 Parish Courts

Approximately 250 Mayor's Courts

Approximately 390 Justices of the Peace

Note: In Capital Cases – where the death penalty has been imposed – appeal is directly to the Supreme Court from the District Court, and in cases where a law has been declared unconstitutional, appeal is directly to the Supreme Court.

Number of Justices and Judges	
Supreme Court	7
Courts of Appeal	53
District, Family and Juvenile	238
City and Parish	73
Total	371

[Data courtesy Office of Judicial Administration, Supreme Court of Louisiana, 2002]

Figure 3.2

The Federal Court System

U.S. SUPREME COURT

- The High Court in Washington, D.C.
- 9 Justices, one of whom is Chief Justice
- Hears appeals from the Supreme Courts of 50 states, Puerto Rico, and U.S. Courts of Appeals

U.S. Judicial Circuit Courts

- 12 Intermediate Appeals Courts
- 1 Court of Appeals for the Federal Circuit
- Hear appeals from U.S. District Courts, Special Courts, and Administrative Agencies

1. Maine, Massachusetts, New Hampshire, Rhode Island, and Puerto Rico
2. Connecticut, New York, Vermont
3. Delaware, Pennsylvania, New Jersey, and U.S. Virgin Islands
4. Maryland, N. Carolina, S. Carolina, Virginia, W.Virginia
5. Louisiana, Mississippi, Texas
6. Kentucky, Michigan, Ohio, Tennessee
7. Illinois, Indiana, Wisconsin
8. Arkansas, Iowa, Minnesota, Missouri, Nebraska, N. Dakota, S. Dakota
9. Alaska, Arizona, California, Hawaii, Idaho, Montana, Nevada, Oregon, and Guam
10. Colorado, Kansas, New Mexico, Oklahoma, Utah, Wyoming
11. Alabama, Florida, Georgia
12. D.C. Circuit
- Court of Appeals for Federal Circuit (in D.C.)

The Thirteen Federal Judicial Courts

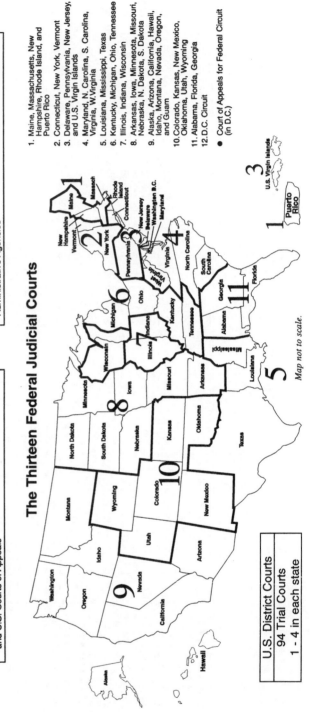

Map not to scale.

U.S. District Courts	94 Trial Courts
	1 - 4 in each state

case may enter the criminal court system as the result of an **arrest**, made either at the scene of a crime or after a report of a crime and an investigation. Usually, once the police have determined there is **probable cause** to believe someone has committed a crime, a **warrant** is obtained from a judge (or in federal court and in some states from a **magistrate**, authorized to conduct more routine proceedings). The warrant is then carried out (**served**); the **suspect** is arrested and brought to the local police station where he is booked into the local jail; his name, address, date and time of arrest, and a description of the circumstances under which he was arrested—as well as, in serious cases, his photograph and fingerprints—may become part of the public record at this point.

Other records—such as confessions—may not be made public. And as most viewers of TV drama know, due to the 1966 US Supreme Court decision *Miranda v Arizona*,[1] at the time of arrest the police must read the suspect his "**Miranda Rule**" rights. These point out he has the right to remain silent; whatever he says may be used against him; and he is entitled to a lawyer, whose services will be provided free if he cannot afford private counsel— either a private lawyer who donates some hours to the state (*pro bono*), or a lawyer paid for by the state (a **public defender**)—or he may choose to represent himself (**pro se**).

In most jurisdictions, the police may detain a suspect in a lockup only for a limited time, generally twenty-four hours, before he is brought into a court for an **initial (first) appearance**. At this time, if the suspect cannot afford a lawyer, the court may appoint someone to represent him. **Bail** may be set. If the suspect makes bail or is granted the right to be released without having to put up a bond (**released on recognizance**, or **ROR**), he may be allowed out of jail, based on the promise he will return for the next step of the judicial process. If the suspect is not granted the opportunity to make bail, or if he is unable to afford the required bail bond, he is returned to jail to await the next step in the judicial process.

At the **arraignment**, taking place in some instances at the **preliminary hearing**, the suspect appears with his lawyer (other lawyers who may assist are designated **of counsel** to the lawyer of record) and is officially charged with a crime. At this point, he is given the opportunity to enter a plea. If he pleads either guilty or *nolo contendere* (**no contest**)—which is a way of accepting the penalty without the actual admission of guilt—or, in some jurisdictions, "guilty but mentally ill"—the penalty may be immediately announced in simple crimes, or a **sentencing** hearing may be scheduled after negotiations between the prosecutor and defense lawyers have been completed. If he pleads not guilty—or, in some states, not guilty by reason of insanity—it will be determined whether there is probable cause to continue the case. If a major felony is charged, in most states the case will likely be **bound over** to a **grand jury**.

The definition of insanity varies. In some jurisdictions, the "**McNaghten (M'Naghten) rule**" still applies. Based on an 1843 case,[2] the defendant is considered insane if he could not tell right from wrong at the time of the crime. However, about half the states today apply the definition from the Model Penal Code: the defendant must lack the "substantial capacity" to "appreciate the criminality of his conduct" and to "conform his conduct to the requirements of law."

The grand jury is a panel made up of a group of citizens—approximately 12–23 in state courts, 16–23 in federal court—convened by the prosecutor, the **district attorney (DA)**, or **state's attorney**. In some states grand juries consider only such issues as government corruption; however, the traditional role of the grand jury is to consider whether there is sufficient evidence to charge a suspect with a serious crime (issue an **indictment**).

A **witness** who receives a **summons** to testify (the name of an actual target is generally written in all caps) is not allowed to bring his lawyer into the grand jury room, although lawyers may wait outside the grand jury room and remain available for consultation with clients. A witness may be granted **immunity** from prosecution in exchange for his testimony. "Use" immunity means the testimony of the witness may not be used against him; "transactional" immunity means the witness may not be prosecuted at all in connection with the offense to which the testimony is related.

The meetings of the grand jury, which considers the prosecutor's recommended charges, are closed to the public and the press. Secrecy is necessary to protect witnesses and particularly to protect the reputations of those who are never charged with any crime.

After listening to all the evidence, the grand jury decides whether to issue an indictment or "**true bill**": if so, the suspect—who likely was one of the grand jury witnesses and may or may not already have been arrested— continues in the judicial process just as if a preliminary hearing had been held after an arrest. Since grand juries hear only from prosecution witnesses, it is understandable that as much as 90 percent of the time, indictments are issued. In a small minority of cases (sometimes, due to resistance to the prosecutor), a "runaway jury" fails to recommend indictment and issues a "**no bill**." Indictments are open to the public and press, although as with the warrant, access may not be available until after an arrest has been made.

In about two-thirds of the states, a prosecutor dealing with a suspect in a noncapital case has another option: he may decide without consulting a grand jury to charge someone with a crime. The charge or official accusation is called an **information** and is treated much the same as a grand jury indictment.

Any one of a number of **motions** (applications to the court for an order to be issued) for pre-trial hearings may be entered at this time. Unless there is so little evidence produced at a hearing that the prosecutor decides to drop the charges (*"nolle prosequi"*), the case continues with the scheduling of pre-trial hearings. A judge is assigned to the case and a trial date is set.

At no time may either side have any *ex parte* (one-sided) contact with the court. If a party needs to speak to the judge, notice to the other side must be given, and the other side must have the opportunity to join in any discussion of the case.

Throughout the pre-trial period, **discovery** continues. In most states, lawyers for both sides may interview potential trial witnesses and record their testimony in a **deposition**. Material thus obtained may be used during the trial, particularly when lawyers wish to attack the credibility of a witness by comparing his trial testimony with his deposition. **Perjury** occurs when someone knowingly makes false statements under oath. Discrediting a witness is referred to as **impeach(ing) the witness**.

Pre-trial hearings may be held for many reasons. For instance, a suspect may object to the introduction of certain evidence and call for a suppression or **exclusionary hearing**. Both the state and federal courts have strict **rules of evidence**, and improper evidence will not be allowed into the trial. For instance, **tainted evidence** is that which has been improperly obtained, such as under a faulty search warrant, and any subsequent evidence resulting from the search would also be **inadmissible** as "**fruit of the poisonous tree**."

A motion *in limine* (pretrial) may ask that certain evidence be excluded because it is sensationalistic, such as gruesome photographs of a murder scene. Such evidence may be so prejudicial the jurors might be overwhelmed with emotion.

Motions may also be made for a delay or **continuance** of the trial or to move the trial to a different location (a **change of venue**) or to isolate (**sequester**) the jury during the trial. Or a motion may be made to **quash** or cancel the indictment for deficiencies in the way it was obtained, such as failure to comply with the "speedy trial" requirements of the Sixth Amendment. A court may agree to order (**subpoena**) the production of certain documents such as the defendant's arrest record or results of physical or mental exams, or to quash or **vacate** such orders due to failure to follow correct procedures. **Stipulations**, or agreements on facts that need not be proven at trial, may be signed by the lawyers for both sides.

In the US today, only a small proportion (estimates range from 5–10 percent) of those charged with a crime actually ever come to trial. In some cases as mentioned above (about a third of the time), the prosecution decides to drop the charges. In the great majority of cases (nearly two-thirds), instead of a trial, the procedure followed is the **plea bargain**, or **negotiated settlement**, an agreement reached by the lawyers for both sides and approved by the judge. In return for pleading guilty to a crime, a defendant has a chance to reduce the charges against him—as well as the concomitant sentence.

Unlike the trial process, much of the plea bargain is closed to the public and press. Instead of the theoretical basis of a trial—**presumption of innocence** with determination of guilt followed by a punishment to fit a crime—the end result of a plea bargain is admission of guilt followed by the selection of a crime to fit a punishment. The lawyers may dismiss some charges and reduce others, and they generally select a charge for which the penalty is less severe than what would have been ordered had the defendant been convicted at trial. The defendant often selects a plea bargain rather than risk the more severe penalty of a **conviction**; the state often accepts a plea bargain rather than risk an **acquittal**—and also to avoid the great expense of a trial. The result of the plea bargain must be approved by a judge at a public hearing.

Another possibility involves a motion to move a suspect into a pre-trial intervention program of some type. (See Figure 3.3: The Pre-Trial Process.)

THE TRIAL

After all the pre-trial hearings have been held, a trial is scheduled (**docketed**). The trial process is familiar since it is the subject of books, television programs, and popular movies. The process is designed to show the guilt or lack of guilt of a defendant charged with committing a crime. In the US, the system theoretically assumes the defendant is not guilty unless the state offers enough evidence to prove his guilt and can convince the jurors of such.

In most jurisdictions, a trial will require a jury in felony cases and those cases in which the penalty exceeds six months in jail, provided the defendant does not waive his right to a jury trial. The first step is to select a jury (a **petit jury** as compared to a grand jury). The pool of potential jurors (*venire*) is drawn from the voter registration lists in about half the states, and in others from a mix of voter lists, the tax rolls, and driver license registration lists.

In a typical situation, the entire *venire* is assigned to appear at the courthouse at the same time, often a Monday morning. Jurors may then be sent to different courtrooms where jury selection is taking place for different trials.

First, the judge will ask those members of the *venire* who may be automatically exempt from jury duty to step forward. At this time, the judge will

Figure 3.3

The Pre-Trial Process

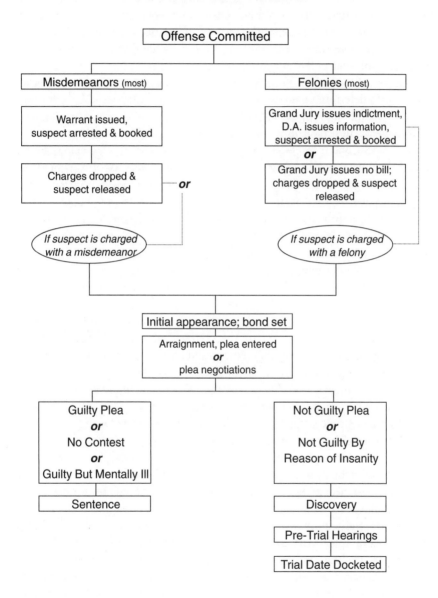

excuse those whose occupations (e.g., lawyers), family situations (such as mothers of infants), or personal situations (such as those in ill health) call for dismissal: the trend today is for fewer such automatic exemptions to be granted. The judge will then ask any others who feel they would be unable to serve on a jury to step forward. For instance, those dismissed may be students during final exam time. The names of those so excused may be returned to the jury pool to be called for future trials.

The remaining members of the *venire* will then face further questioning from the judge (in federal cases) or from lawyers for both sides who will question them, either individually or in groups or **panels**, regarding suitability for serving on a specific jury. This process is called *voir dire*.

A motion may be made to **strike** or dismiss a juror from serving. Jurors may be **challenged for cause**, either general (the juror may not meet minimum requirements such as age), or due to some sort of bias. For instance, the potential juror may be related to one of the participants in the case or may say he would not be able to vote to impose the death penalty in a capital case (questioning of jurors on the death penalty is called **qualifying the jury**). There is usually an unlimited number of such challenges. Each side also has a limited number of **peremptory challenges**, dismissals for reasons that need not be stated at the time, with limits generally tied in with the possible penalty in criminal cases and set by statute in civil cases. However, several recent court cases have held jurors cannot be dismissed if race (the "**Batson test**"[3]), ethnicity, religion, or gender[4] is the prime factor in the decision. The art of picking juries has become highly refined, and often consultants to one or both sides will help the lawyers during voir dire.

The rest of the *venire* is dismissed after the requisite number of jurors has been selected—generally either six or twelve, with one or two alternates who will hear the entire case and will be dismissed if not needed when final deliberations begin. The court may also grant a motion to "**invoke the rule**" on exclusion of witnesses—that is, each witness will be kept out of the courtroom until it is his turn to testify. The court usually allows a day or two for jurors to make arrangements to be away from work or home for the estimated length of the trial.

The trial itself begins with the swearing-in (**impaneling**) of the jury. From this point on, "**jeopardy attaches**," that is, the only way to stop the trial after this is for the judge to declare a mistrial. Following this are **opening statements**, whereby attorneys for each side present outlines of evidence to be presented. After this, the prosecutor presents the **direct evidence**, calling witnesses who offer **testimony** favoring the state's case. Fact witnesses must have firsthand knowledge regarding their testimony; only **expert witnesses**, after proving they are qualified to be so designated, may offer opinions regarding the case.

The defense is permitted to question each witness during **cross-examination**—however, questions may deal only with material covered in the direct examination. Then the prosecution may recall any earlier witnesses ("**redirect**") and the defense then has the opportunity to "**re-cross**" before the prosecution rests its case. Testimony may include direct eyewitness accounts as well as **circumstantial evidence**—that which is merely implied from direct evidence (and that jurors later may be instructed to weigh less heavily than direct evidence).

The defense may put on an **affirmative defense**, in which rather than deny the charges, the claim is made of police misconduct, self-defense, or other factors that would mean the defendant is not criminally responsible for the act. Whatever the approach, lawyers are trained not to ask any witness a question to which they do not know the answer ahead of time—they have "**prepared**" (rehearsed) their own witnesses, prosecution or defense, prior to trial.

Throughout the trial, from opening statements through closing arguments, lawyers for either side may **object** to various procedures and to certain evidence. For instance, a lawyer's opening statements may be seen as arguing the case or offering personal opinions. Evidence may be objected to as improper, immaterial, or irrelevant—that is, in some manner inappropriate and therefore inadmissible. It may be **hearsay**, or secondhand testimony, and not meet any of the possible hearsay exemptions. Or perhaps during direct examination the opposing lawyer is **leading the witness**, asking a question that strongly suggests the desired answer. Or the evidence may represent the opinion of the witness rather than facts (only expert witnesses, as mentioned, may offer opinions).

Other objections to testimony include charges it is ambiguous, "argumentative," assumes facts not in evidence, is confusing or misleading, calls for a narrative answer, is repetitious, nonresponsive, speculative, vague, or beyond the scope of the case. In an improper "**speaking objection**," the lawyer tries to work in hints to the witness as to the best way to answer the question if the objection is overruled.

The judge may choose to uphold (**sustain**) an objection and strike the testimony from the record or to **overrule** it, allowing the testimony to stand. Whatever the court rules, the lawyer who "lost" on his motion may in some jurisdictions file an **exception for the record** that will make his disagreement with the court a formal part of the record in order to preserve it in case the verdict is appealed. Or if an objection to evidence is sustained, the lawyer who is overruled may make an **offer of proof** whereby in the absence of the jury, a lawyer dictates the testimony he expected from the witness in order to make the evidence part of the record. At any rate, lawyers make many motions, because if they do not complain at the time of the alleged offense and enter it into the official record, they cannot complain at the time of appeal.

Lawyers may ask to "**approach the bench**" to speak to the judge privately in a **sidebar** or **bench conference**, or the judge may suggest they move to his chambers, where certain issues can be discussed privately (*in camera*). For example, one issue discussed might be a request to **proffer** (offer) evidence to be presented so the judge might rule on its admissibility.

Throughout the proceedings, the judge will frequently **admonish** the jurors not to discuss the case with anyone nor to follow press coverage. This is to avoid prejudicing the jurors.

At the conclusion of the presentation of the prosecution's evidence, after the prosecution **rests**, each side will make motions, generally outside the presence of the jury. The defense attorney may make a motion for a **judgment of acquittal** or **JOA**, requesting an immediate acquittal based on his claim the state has failed to prove its case. The judge may grant such motions, deny them, or reserve ruling for later in the trial.

During the second half of the trial, the defense has the opportunity to present its own evidence and its own witnesses. The prosecution has the right to cross-examine any witnesses on issues brought up during the direct testimony, and the re-cross by the defense is similar to that followed by the prosecution in the first half of the trial. Furthermore, the prosecution is allowed to recall earlier witnesses and even to call **rebuttal witnesses** to refute testimony offered by the defense witnesses. In some cases, the defense may then offer a **rejoinder** to contradict the rebuttal. The defendant may or may not choose to testify on his own behalf before the defense rests its case. One consideration is that certain evidence, ordinarily inadmissible—such as a record of prior convictions—may be admissible only if the defendant takes the stand. At any rate, the Fifth Amendment provides a privilege against self-incrimination.

After the defense rests, the lawyers may again make motions such as another defense motion for a directed verdict, but these are usually denied. Then the **closing arguments** or **summations** are offered, as the lawyers sum up the positions of their clients. Unlike opening statements, closing arguments are designed to advocate a defendant's guilt or lack of guilt. However, lawyers may not bring up new evidence or comment on the failure of a defendant to have testified in his own defense. They should not offer personal opinions, appeal to personal prejudice, or attack the motives of the other lawyers. The prosecutor argues first and may rebut the defense's closing argument, on the theory the state has the more difficult position since it bears the burden of proof of guilt.

At this point, the judge will **instruct** or **charge the jury** with guidelines to follow in its deliberations. These instructions are the result of meetings with lawyers for both sides, and although the general formula is the same in most cases involving similar criminal charges throughout the state, the lawyers are concerned with which specific details are included or excluded. The instructions will define legal terms and will remind the jurors of the presumption of innocence, the fact the lawyers' questions and statements were not evidence, and the jurors' duty not to speculate on inadmissible evidence to which objections were sustained. The instructions may become part of the grounds for an appeal in case of a conviction, if it is charged the judge or the instructions confused the jury or otherwise led to a faulty verdict.

At any rate, in criminal cases the **burden of proof** is on the state to prove the defendant's guilt **beyond a reasonable doubt**—each juror must have an abiding conviction, or in some jurisdictions a moral certainty, that the defendant is guilty. Some further define this standard as proof of such a convincing nature that you would be willing to rely and act upon it without hesitation in the most important of your own affairs.

After instructing the jury, the judge will send jurors to a separate room to deliberate: while they are deliberating, no one may enter the room or in any way **tamper** with the jury. The jury members may take evidence with them and may ask questions of the judge via the bailiff.

After deliberations are concluded, the jury will return to the courtroom and present its **verdict**. Or the jury may be **deadlocked**, that is, simply unable to agree on a verdict. If a unanimous jury is required, as it is in most federal cases and major felony cases, the **hung jury** will cause the judge to declare a **mistrial**, and in most cases a new trial will be scheduled. Other matters that might lead to a mistrial include the death of someone closely related to the case such as a key witness, or the misconduct of a lawyer in the case or the granting of a motion for a mistrial made by the defense.

If the jury **finds** the defendant **not guilty**, the defendant is usually immediately released from custody. Acquittals occur about one-fifth of the time. The state generally has no right to appeal an acquittal, although it may appeal certain issues of law or perceived errors, and in convictions the length of a sentence. Due to the protections against **double jeopardy** offered by the US Constitution, the acquitted defendant cannot be tried by the same court a second time on the same criminal charges.

If the defendant is found **guilty** or convicted, he may request the jury be **polled**, and each juror must announce aloud his agreement with the verdict. About four-fifths of the time, a defendant is convicted in a jury trial. Occasionally a defiant jury will acquit a defendant despite evidence of guilt or, more rarely, vice versa. This is often referred to as **jury nullification**. A sentencing hearing may be scheduled for a few hours, days, or even weeks after the conclusion of the trial.

At the time of the verdict, the losing side may file a motion for a **judgment *non obstante verdicto*** or **n.o.v.** (**"notwithstanding the verdict"**), asking the judge for a favorable ruling based on the evidence, in spite of what the jury decided. Or a defendant may move for a new trial, although such motions are rarely granted. Once the judge accepts the verdict it becomes official, and unless the jury is needed for sentencing, it is dismissed, and the convicted defendant is returned to jail to await sentencing. (See Figure 3.4: The Trial Process.)

POST-TRIAL PROCEEDINGS

After a conviction, the court may order an investigation into the defendant's background and may order a report to the court at the time the sentencing hearing is scheduled: the report itself is generally not available to the public ahead of time. At the hearing, the report may be read and various witnesses may testify as to the character of the defendant and any aggravating circumstances (**evidence in mitigation**) that should be taken into consideration. Victim(s) of the crime(s) committed by the defendant(s) may testify, as may families of the victim, and the defendant may make statements on his own behalf.

The judge announces the sentence, based on the report and in accord with the state's **sentencing guidelines**. Fixed or **determinate sentences** require a set fine, a definite number of years in prison, or both; **indeterminate sentences** include a range of penalties. Sentences on multiple charges may be **concurrent** (combining the number of years to run simultaneously) or **consecutive** (with years added together to lengthen the sentence). Or the sentence may be **suspended** and the defendant put on **probation** wherein he is required to meet certain conditions such as community service, working for no pay for the public good at a designated place.

The defense must file appeals in a **timely** fashion. That is, the defense has only a limited period of time from the conviction in which to file its **notices of appeal**, which are filed in about one-tenth of felony cases and automatically in capital cases. The defendant becomes the **appellant**, and the state becomes the **appellee**: the defendant's name is now listed first when the case is appealed, and the burden of proof shifts to the defendant. The court prepares a record of the trial, and the lawyers file **briefs** based on the record.

Figure 3.4

The Trial Process

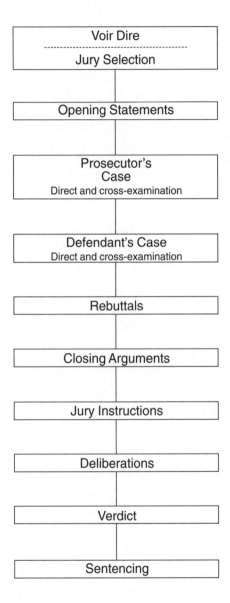

Unlike the sequence in the trial court, in the appellate court the defendant usually has the last word, whether written or oral, since the burden of proof has shifted from the prosecution. The appellate court does not re-try the case but reviews only the trial process, considering points of law or perhaps the severity of the sentence. The record of the trial, briefs from each party, and in some cases short oral arguments are all that is considered by an appellate court. During this time, the defendant generally remains imprisoned and does not appear at the hearing, although this depends on the seriousness of the crime. The decision regarding the appeal may be handed down by the higher court several weeks or more likely months after the trial.

The appeal courts in most states are made up of groups of judges. The entire group meeting *en banc* may consider an appeal, or it may be heard by a committee or **panel** of judges. State courts may have as few as three judges on an appellate court while a federal appeal court may have as many as twenty-six judges: a three-judge panel is common. Federal courts hear about 35,000 appeals per year.

The opinion or holding of the appeal court is generally issued in writing. One judge writes for the majority; another may write a **dissent**. A third judge may **concur** with the majority holding but state different reasons for doing so. Or the court may issue a *per curium* ("**by the court**") decision, often without explaining its reasons. At this point, the case is finally resolved unless further appeals are filed. Unlike most trial court decisions, the holdings of appellate courts are available to the public in bound volumes called "reporters" in law libraries and computerized data bases such as Lexis and Westlaw.

If, as happens about 95 percent of the time, the appellate court has upheld or **affirmed** the trial court's conviction despite any minor **harmless errors**, the defendant may ask for a re-hearing or in some cases may appeal the case to a state's high court. State supreme court judges generally vote *en banc*. Appeals from an intermediate to a high court follow the same basic process as appeals from a trial court to an intermediate appellate court.

In the rare instances in which a criminal conviction is overturned due to serious or **reversible error** made by trial courts, the appellate court may **reverse** the lower court decision, may **set aside** the decision, and may order the lower court to render a new decision. Or the higher court may **remand** the case to the lower court for another trial—a trial *de novo*, which is held as if the first trial never took place.

Most defendants sentenced do serve time in prison, although those convicted of serious crimes may end up spending only 25–30 percent of the time originally imposed due to various ways of earning **gain time**, days off the sentence. (See Figure 3.5: The Appeal Process.)

The federal high court, the US Supreme Court—the only court actually

Figure 3.5

The Appeal Process

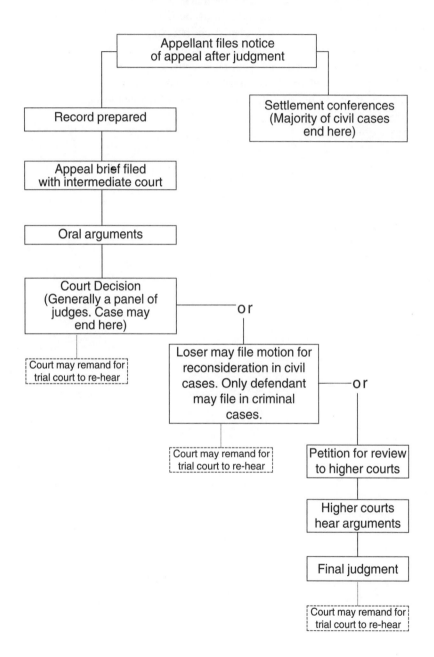

mandated by the federal Constitution—hears some cases of original jurisdiction (e.g., when an ambassador is a party), but generally may hear an appeal only after the defendant has exhausted all appeals in his home state. Contrary to popular view, only certain cases may be appealed to the US Supreme Court. All nine US Supreme Court **justices** hear appeals *en banc*. Only about half of the 100 or so cases that they vote to hear each year (out of 5,000 requests) are criminal appeals from state courts. At least four justices must vote to issue a ***writ of certiorari*** agreeing to hear an appeal.

The above description is applicable to a case followed through the criminal process. The differences in a case followed through the civil courts are addressed in chapter 4.

NOTES

1. *Miranda v Arizona*, 384 US 436 (1966).
2. *McNaghten's (M'Naghten's) Case*, 8 Eng Rep 718 (1843).
3. *Batson v Kentucky*, 476 US 79 (1986).
4. See, for example, *JEB v Alabama*, 511 US 127 (1994).

Chapter Four

Civil Procedure

"The bad news is we're being sued. The good news is they're letting us televise the trial."

A case usually enters the civil court system when one party files a **complaint** or **petition** against another over some alleged wrong. The complaint describes the reasons the plaintiff feels the court has jurisdiction over a case and sets out the demand for relief.

The plaintiff in a civil case must prove someone acted contrary to law and that this act, or **cause of action**, directly caused him injury from which he has a right to recover. The plaintiff may "pray for" a remedy such as an **injunction** that halts or **enjoins** some behavior by the respondent: a **temporary restraining order (TRO)** may be issued before a hearing. Or the plaintiff may simply request a **declaratory ruling**, asking the court to issue an opinion as to who has rights regarding a certain action.

Many times the plaintiff is seeking monetary **damages**: **actual** or **compensatory damages** cover the out-of-pocket expenses of the plaintiff, while **punitive damages** are designed to punish the defendant (or "respondent"). For instance, the case may involve a person in the news who sues a newspaper because he feels the paper has falsely defamed him: this is libel, a type of

tort or wrong inflicted by one party on another. Or the case may involve breach of a **contract** or agreement between two parties.

THE CIVIL TRIAL

After the respondent is served with the complaint, either by a sheriff's deputy, by certified mail, or by a notice posted in a daily newspaper, he has a specific time period in which to file an **answer**. The respondent may file a **counterclaim** with his answer and the plaintiff may then file a **reply** to the answer or counterclaim. Or the respondent may file a **demurrer**, saying even if the facts in the complaint are true, the plaintiff has no legal cause of action to bring a case or lacks **standing**, the right to bring the action. Or the respondent may claim the issue is moot, not open for legal consideration. Other affirmative defenses in a civil case include the failure of a plaintiff to bring a case within the statute of limitations, or a claim the issue has already been settled and need not be re-opened (*res judicata*). Or the respondent may file a **special appearance**, notice that he acknowledges the receipt of the complaint but contends the court lacks the **jurisdiction** necessary to hear the case. If no answer is filed, the plaintiff may win by default.

Outside parties may file to become involved in the case as *amicus curiae*, or **intervenors**. (More often, *amicus* file an appeal brief after an adverse decision.)

Discovery proceeds much as it does in a criminal trial, although the defendant will have to testify, since the Fifth Amendment privilege applies only to criminal cases. Witnesses give depositions, testifying in meetings with lawyers for both sides. During the depositions, clients may be advised by lawyers not to answer certain questions, and opposing lawyers may object, just as they do in court. Often the opposing lawyer will make a standing objection to all questions of a certain type; the client may go ahead and answer them, and the judge will be asked to rule on their admissibility if and when the deposition testimony becomes part of the case.

Pre-trial conferences and hearings are held; participants may sign **affidavits** (sworn testimony). Lawyers may ask witnesses to answer written lists of questions (**interrogatories**) and may issue **requests for admission**, which require responses to written statements that the respondent must either admit or deny. Or the court may be asked to order or subpoena witnesses to produce documentary evidence. **Best evidence** is primary material such as originals of documents rather than photocopies.

Certain issues on which the parties agree may lead to stipulations. Either party may ask the judge to dismiss the case, or the judge may order the parties to enter **mediation**—an out-of-court process of resolving conflict in which a mediator counsels both sides in an attempt to reach some compromise prior to final court action. When the parties have completed all the **pleadings** and have narrowed the case to specific issues of disagreement, they are said to be **at issue**, ready for trial.

And just as the great majority of criminal cases are settled with plea bargaining, most civil cases, perhaps 90 percent, are settled prior to a full trial. Often the terms of the **settlement**, which generally must be approved by a judge, are sealed from the public in a civil case, often at the request of the parties such as in a heated divorce.

At any time before the trial, a party in a civil case may ask the judge for a **summary judgment**, wherein one party attempts to convince the court there are no issues of material fact, and thus that side feels it is entitled to prevail as a matter of law. More often than not, however, in the minority of cases that are not settled pre-trial, the summary judgment will not be granted either, and the case will go to trial.

If a civil case does reach the trial stage, often after years of pre-trial litigation, the trial process is analogous to that of a criminal trial. The case may be heard as a **jury trial** or by the judge alone (a **bench trial**). The Seventh Amendment provides the right to a jury trial when the amount in question is more than $20. The bench trial is generally shorter since the judge, who is already familiar with the case, might not need to hear opening statements or closing arguments. Often a judge will wait some time after the trial before issuing his judgment: this is referred to as "taking the matter under advisement."

Like the criminal prosecutor, the plaintiff's lawyer in a civil case presents his case first: direct evidence, cross-examination, re-cross, and various motions follow. One common motion in a civil case is a **motion to dismiss** wherein the judge is asked to declare insufficient evidence has been presented for an adverse finding. If the case is dismissed "**with prejudice**," it means it may not be re-filed.

The second half of the trial includes a similar procedure followed by the respondent's lawyer. Often in the midst of a civil trial a judge will issue some type of temporary order, called an **interlocutory** order, requiring some action by a trial participant before the trial proceeds.

Just as in a criminal case where a lawyer may move for a judgment of acquittal, during the trial in a civil case a lawyer may move for a **directed verdict**, a finding for one side or the other based on the evidence prior to the jury's deliberation or the completion of testimony in a bench trial. Or a judge may order a directed verdict on his own initiative.

In contrast to the criminal trial's requirement that the state must prove its case beyond a reasonable doubt, the burden of proof in a civil case is either a **preponderance of the evidence** (more convincing weight of the argument) or **clear and convincing evidence** (highly probable, somewhere in between "beyond a reasonable doubt" and a "preponderance of the evidence"). In some civil cases, the jury may be charged only with deciding the facts, and the judge will apply the law to the facts.

It is likely the jury verdict in a civil case will require only a three-fourths or five-sixths vote. As will be recalled, this contrasts with the unanimous votes required in many criminal cases.

As in a criminal trial, the verdict of the jury or the decision of the judge finding either for the plaintiff (in which case the defendant/respondent is described as found **liable** rather than "convicted") or in favor of the defendant/respondent may be appealed. Unlike the criminal trial, in which the state generally cannot appeal an acquittal, in a civil trial either side (or both, in a **cross-appeal**) may appeal the decision. In a civil case, the appeal may be carried through at least one higher court in most cases. (See Figure 4.1: The Civil Process.)

FEDERAL COURTS AND SPECIAL
COURT PROCEEDINGS

In general, most court proceedings, whether civil or criminal, are similar whether the activity takes place in a state court (where more than 95 percent of cases are heard) or in a federal court. Jurisdiction of the case depends on several factors. For instance, civil cases in which each of the parties is from a different state (**diversity of citizenship**) and in which monetary damages sought are substantial (usually more than $75,000) may be heard in a federal court. In such cases, the court may follow the laws of the state in which the case is brought (generally the home state of the party who filed first) or those of the state in which it sits.

Some issues generally heard in federal courts include controversies involving foreign governments or disputes between states, as well as antitrust actions, bankruptcies, civil rights issues, copyright cases (assigned to federal courts by the US Constitution), election disputes, and cases involving immigration. Federal criminal issues generally include those involving counterfeiting, narcotics, and racketeering.

Each of the ninety-four federal districts is headed by a **US attorney** who may have as many as fifty assistants. Unlike most state district attorneys, US attorneys are appointed rather than elected. And although judges in most state courts are elected or chosen by a combination of appointment and election,

Figure 4.1

The Civil Process

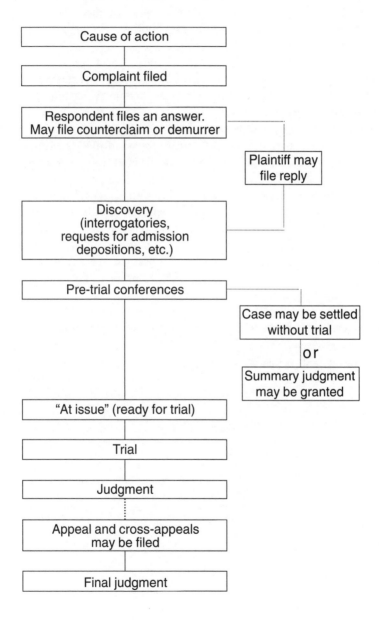

judges in federal courts are appointed via a highly partisan political process: they are nominated by the president and must be confirmed by the Congress.

Some procedural differences from state courts should also be noted. For instance, it is often the judge alone, or the judge in conjunction with the lawyers, who conducts the *voir dire* in federal courts. Also, there are generally fewer pre-trial hearings than in state courts.

Procedures followed in special courts are for the most part similar to those followed in general courts. For instance, a state may institute special trial courts ranging from justice of the peace courts and magistrate courts to those hearing only special matters—traffic courts, small claims courts, family courts, juvenile courts, and probate courts. Similarly, special federal courts include claims courts, international trade courts, military courts, and tax courts. Many regulatory agencies such as the Federal Communications Commission (FCC) also have court-like tribunals.

In some cases, conflict resolution may be handled completely outside the court system in some type of **alternative dispute resolution**. Or a case may start off in a civil court but be moved to a nonjudicial forum. **Arbitration** is one alternative for dispute resolution. A referee is appointed, and both sides are bound ahead of time to follow his suggestions. In **mediation**, a mediator counsels both sides in an attempt to reach a compromise. Another alternative is a **summary jury trial**, whereby a mock jury hears the facts and the "verdict" helps the parties design a settlement.

However, since the majority of cases covered by the press are criminal cases, it is necessary to take a detailed look at the coverage of criminal cases—the subject of chapter 5.

Chapter Five

Criminal Cases: Pre-Trial Coverage

" I TRIED, BUT WITH ALL THE HIGH-PROFILE
CASES GOING ON, I JUST CAN'T GET YOU
ANY PREJUDICIAL PRE-TRIAL PUBLICITY."

As discussed in chapter 2, fewer than 10 percent of criminal cases and a similarly small minority of civil cases ever proceed to trial. Thus, a journalist must be prepared to devote much of his energy to covering pre-trial activities, including police and court actions, grand jury proceedings, pre-trial hearings, and plea bargains. Then, if a trial is actually held, the journalist will be well prepared to present intelligent coverage.

ACCESS TO RECORDS

Along with the aforementioned First and Sixth Amendment rights of freedom of the press and the right of the accused to a fair public trial, both federal and state access laws require much of the activity of government be presumed open to the public. Journalists serve as the conduit for information available to the public, so the journalist has an obligation to make every attempt to provide the fullest possible coverage of the judicial system.

In criminal cases, most records are available from the time of an arrest. A journalist may learn of an arrest through listening to the police radio, from tips from contacts, or from routine checking with the police. Most jurisdictions provide some type of **"police blotter"** or **jailbook**—a chronological log that includes the name and address of each suspect along with the date, time, and place of arrest along with booking information such as property taken from the suspect at time of arrest. Attached will be the complaint or probable cause affidavit stating the basis for the suspicion of illegal activity regarding which the suspect was arrested. Also, the police will keep a record of whether the arrest was made in connection with a warrant signed by a judge that allows for the search and arrest, as well as a copy of the **return**—a record of what action was taken under the warrant.

The blotter is generally open to the public and the press, as are most warrants once they are served. However, as with court records, parts of police records may be **redacted**, that is, the record may be altered to conceal certain information such as names of confidential informants.

Since warrants often become a matter of some controversy (remember the question of whether police had obtained a warrant before searching the property of OJ Simpson after his wife and her friend were found murdered?), it might be a good idea for you to take notes in case the material is subsequently sealed. Particularly useful are names and addresses mentioned in the warrant.

You might also photograph the warrants themselves once they are available, for use in initial stories regarding an arrest or for later trial coverage.

In both criminal and civil cases, a chronological record of court activity—the docket—is available to the public. A journalist who routinely checks the docket will find it a valuable source of tips. Once a journalist decides he is interested in a case, he can obtain specific case files from the clerk of the court. In a criminal case, files are usually kept by the defendant's last name, or the material may be arranged chronologically.

The **caption** or heading of the file will give the court ID number and title of the case, the names of the litigants, and the date the case began. The file will include discovery material and all records compiled to date such as any motions filed. In a murder case, the file may include details of the autopsy report. Obviously the files are a rich source of material for the journalist.

In dealing with access to records in the federal courts, the journalist should be aware of the US Department of Justice Media Relations Guidelines. These attempt to balance fair trial and free press interests with the government's ability to appropriately administer justice. (See appendix B.)

Juvenile records present a special case: the *Federal Juvenile Delinquency Act* creates a presumption that most juvenile court proceedings be closed to the public. The Reporters Committee for Freedom of the Press (RCFP) periodically publishes excellent guides to juvenile justice as well as to judicial records in general.[1]

*A good journalist will become very friendly with people who work in the clerk's office.

Some trial records may be available online. Both Westlaw's West Doc (www.westdoc.com) and Lexis's Lexis One (lexisone.com) maintain extensive databases for a fee. FindLaw (www.findlaw.com) provides free access to some cases as well as links to pay services such as PACER (Public Access to Court Electronic Records, www.pacer.psc.uscourt.gov) that provides access to federal court records. PACER currently provides up to $10 a year of free access and charges seven cents a page thereafter. Court TV Online (www.courttv.com) is a free service that includes archival information, video clips, and breaking news on cases covered.

In 2000, the National Center for State Courts (NCSC) set up an online information clearinghouse (ncsc.online.org) with links to state and federal websites as well as information on public access to court records and related data privacy issues. However, several press organizations argued that the NCSC-proposed Model Policy on Public Access to Court Records would replace the presumption of openness with an arbitrary "balancing test" including privacy and copyright issues.[2]

In 2001, the US Judicial Conference—the twenty-seven-member governing body on federal courts—voted to allow online access to certain civil case files and, in 2002, to allow online access to records in high-profile criminal cases such as those involving the suspects in the September 11 terrorist attacks. The conference also voted to initiate a pilot program (in one appeal court and ten trial courts) for online access to criminal case records on a regular basis.[3]

The press is often successful in obtaining access to court records if access motions are filed.[4] However, many times despite continued attempts, the press fails to win access. One of the most egregious examples was the 2000 trial of four-time former Louisiana Governor Edwin Edwards and six others on charges of fraud in the issuance of riverboat casino licenses. In that case, almost all 1,500 records remained sealed until after the trial ended, including, initially, the press's motions to unseal the records.[5]

Journalists who legally obtain documents sealed by the court may sometimes publish without challenge. However, media lawyers remind you of the hazards of publishing a document you have obtained legally when an order has been directed to the press forbidding publication.[6]

It should be noted that state judges are encouraged to support access to courts. As *Managing Notorious Trials*, the judges' handbook published by the National Center for State Courts, quotes one of the judges interviewed: "The most important thing to the media is that they have access. A judge either accommodates the press or fights with them." Later, the handbook reminds judges that when it comes to court records, "Access cannot be denied except for compelling countervailing reasons."[7]

If you are still denied access to records you feel should be public, put your request into writing, identifying the records requested.
After a refusal, you should respectfully request a denial in writing. Sometimes this will lead to a clerk's change of attitude—or at least you will create a paper trail to refer to if you then seek the assistance of the paper's or station's legal counsel. Most challenges in recent years—albeit those reported by the press itself—have been successful.

GRAND JURY PROCEEDINGS

In criminal cases, a suspect in most serious cases will likely have entered the judicial process as the result of a "true bill" or indictment by a grand jury. If the jury had issued a "no bill," no charges would have been filed. (As mentioned earlier, a grand jury report on general issues such as corruption is a **presentment**, and may or may not include any indictments.)

As discussed in chapter 2, the work of the grand jury is not open to the public, and anyone attempting even to photograph a member of the grand jury or a witness entering or leaving the grand jury room may be subject to a **contempt** citation, in which the court orders someone punished with a fine, jail term, or both. However, the names of the grand jurors may be available in the clerk's office.

Grand jury witnesses are generally allowed to describe their own testimony; there can be no restraints on such descriptions after the grand jury has finished its work and issued its finding. In many jurisdictions, including federal court, witnesses are not prohibited from talking to reporters, although reporters writing stories on grand jury proceedings are subject to subpoena if they rely on unnamed sources. The law on access to ancillary proceedings to grand jury investigations is unsettled, as brought out by the 1998 controversies over access to information regarding President Clinton, Monica Lewinsky, and Paula Jones.[8]

The actual target of the grand jury investigation (the one whose name is written in all capital letters usually is the target; the rest of those subpoenaed are witnesses) may not be subpoenaed to testify. However, the district attorney may send the target a letter inviting him to testify; anyone may decline such an invitation without being subject to contempt charges.

*Since the grand jury is generally seen as a tool of the prosecution, you would want to maintain close contact with the district attorney and be prepared for an immediate interview as soon as the grand jury is dismissed. As discussed, in some jurisdictions the DA himself may substitute his charge, the information, for the indictment, giving you even more reason to remain on good terms with his office.
*If you report "leaked" information about grand jury actions, it is possible you will be subpoenaed and ordered to reveal your source for the information or be found in contempt. (A **subpoena** *duces tecum requires you not only to appear in court but also to bring certain material—your notes, even outtakes of videotapes—with you or face contempt charges.)*

Grand jury indictments are generally open to the public. However, the indictment will be sealed if there is some compelling reason, such as the government's fear that the suspect might flee. As soon as the suspect is arrested, however, the indictment and other records generally become open.

HEARINGS AND PLEA BARGAINS

As discussed, after a suspect in a criminal case is arrested and booked by the police, he is detained until some sort of initial appearance, followed by arraignment, indictment, and preliminary hearings. The scheduling of these procedures is docketed in advance and usually available to the public.

These early pre-trial actions are a good place for you to talk to families of suspects and victims in a criminal case—later their lawyers may advise them not to talk to members of the press.

There are numerous reasons a litigant might file pre-trial motions that require a hearing. In a criminal case, these include motions for dismissals, continuances, bond hearings, and exclusionary hearings. In a civil case, they include motions for summary judgment and requests for discovery material. Since much may depend on what is decided in these hearings, the alert journalist would want to be present when possible.

Two particularly significant types of hearings are dismissals and exclusionary hearings. In federal court, these decisions may be made without oral arguments, but in most state courts the issues must be argued before a judge. Suppression hearings are particularly sensitive, since they often deal with material that the defense hopes will be ruled inadmissible at the trial. And defense attorneys are often wary about the presence of the press at these hearings.

If you discover a hearing is scheduled to be held, and the court has announced ahead of time it will be a closed hearing, after discussing the issue with your editor or news director, you should immediately send the judge a written objection and ask the judge to allow arguments for openness to be held prior to the hearing.

If it appears a judge or magistrate is about to close a hearing, you should contact your editor or news director and possibly the organization's legal counsel to help you argue in court that the hearing be allowed to remain open.

If there is no time to send for help, you might ask someone to call your office while you stand in court and read respectfully, and then hand to the clerk a statement prepared by your news organization such as the following:

> May it please the court (or "Your Honor"):
> My name is _____ and I work for _____ (name of organization). On behalf of myself and my employer, I object to the proposed closing of this proceeding. Although I am not a lawyer, I understand the public has a constitutional right of access to court proceedings. I therefore respectfully request that a hearing be held with my lawyer present before these proceedings are closed. Thank you.

If the judge refuses to hold a hearing on openness, before you leave the courtroom you should request the judge issue a written order closing the proceeding.

Most of the time, your legal counsel would suggest you not agree to any

"deals" with the court such as your being allowed to stay at a hearing if you agree not to produce any report on it.
*No matter what: if a judge orders you to leave a courtroom, obey the court!

As with access to court records, the press is often successful when filing suit to obtain access to court hearings, as in the 2001 murder arraignment of Michael Skakel, a nephew of Robert F. Kennedy.[9] One judge, apologizing for having closed the arraignment of a state representative on charges relating to the death of a man struck by a vehicle, said: "The exclusion of the press from the arraignment court yesterday was totally without justification. The press should have free and unfiltered access to all public proceedings in our courts."[10]

Also similar to the issue of court records, the judges' handbook for covering high-profile cases encourages access to proceedings: "All hearings, including pretrial hearings, should be conducted in court rather than by telephone. Frequent sidebars and *in camera* discussions should be avoided if at all possible."[11]

At any point, a judge may also issue a **"gag order"** or **restrictive order** on trial participants including the lawyers and witnesses, ordering them not to speak to anyone outside the court about the case. Such orders are generally upheld when they apply to courtroom participants such as lawyers. However, as mentioned in chapter 2, when similar restrictions are issued against the press, these are often regarded as unconstitutional prior restraints, so if this situation should arise, a journalist immediately should contact legal counsel for advice on requesting a hearing to remove the restriction. Several press organizations may also be helpful; for instance, the Reporters Committee for Freedom of the Press maintains a First Amendment Hotline.[12]

The press is often successful in challenging gag orders, as in cases reaching the Arkansas and New Mexico Supreme Courts.[13] And in a 2002 case in Georgia involving an investigation of the operator of a crematorium held in connection with the finding of more than 300 corpses, the press was successful in at least modifying the gag, limiting it to public officials.[14]

However, there has been a disturbing trend developing since 1976 when the US Supreme Court decision in the Nebraska case (discussed in chapter 2) discouraged judges from issuing gag orders against the press: many times judges issue gag orders against the trial participants, a de facto gag against reporters who are unable to conduct interviews. As mentioned in chapter 1, the media were unsuccessful in attempts to lift gags in *McVeigh*, and Monica Lewinsky was bound by a gag order under the terms of immunity with prosecutors. Gag orders were upheld in the 2001 murder trial of Andrea Yates, convicted of drowning her five children,[15] and in proceedings in the 2002 case of the man convicted with the murder of seven-year-old Danielle Van Dam in California (although the Van Dam trial was televised live on Court TV).[16]

One of the most egregious examples was the gag on trial participants in the Edwards case mentioned above as well as in an insurance fraud case involving both Edwards and Louisiana Insurance Commissioner Jim Brown. The US Fifth Circuit upheld the gag in the Brown case despite the fact the motion to object came from the defendant himself.[17]

Again, judges are reminded by the handbook on handling high-profile trials that they should seek voluntary compliance with ABA standards and local disciplinary rules: "Gag orders, sanctions, or other means to force compliance should be used sparingly."[18]

Also, at any point pre-trial, a criminal defendant may agree to a plea bargain. Generally the deal-making process itself is conducted in private. Lawyers for the prosecution and the defense work together to determine just what penalty would be fair for the defendant, based on such factors as the seriousness of the crime, the record of the defendant, and the circumstances under which the crime was committed. In a reversal of the common understanding of the judicial process, the negotiators then select a crime to fit the punishment, i.e., a crime for which the sentencing guidelines call for a penalty deemed acceptable. For example, a defendant faced with first-degree murder might find the charges reduced to second-degree murder, whereby the sentence might call for twenty-five years in prison rather than a possible life sentence or even a death penalty were the case to proceed to a conviction at trial.

The defendant must agree to plead guilty to the crime selected, and the parties must then schedule a hearing where lawyers for both sides as well as the defendant himself must appear before the trial judge for his approval. The journalist might not learn of the plea bargain until it is presented in open court. If the judge should fail to approve of the plea agreement—which rarely occurs—the defendant may re-instate a not guilty plea, and the case will proceed to trial.

There seems to be an increase in the number of requests by journalists for more access to the plea bargaining process. You might ask the lawyers to let you know if they are close to an agreement so you can present more comprehensive coverage.

Several cases in which the results of a plea bargain have been sealed have been appealed by the press with some success. It cannot hurt to try.[19]

Plea-bargaining is an excellent subject for an enterprise story. You might describe the extent of the practice in your jurisdiction and interview participants of a particular case including judges, lawyers, and litigants. Interviews with crime victims can also be instructive.

As discussed, a low percentage of cases makes it to this point in the judicial process, the trial: estimates are that charges are dropped in nearly a third of criminal cases and plea bargains approved in nearly two-thirds. However, cases in which the prosecution in a criminal case is convinced of the likelihood of success—or some extremely notorious cases—do proceed to trial. And it is the trial itself that is of greatest interest to journalists, and the subject of discussion in chapter 6.

NOTES

1. See, for example, Reporters Committee for Freedom of the Press (RCFP), *Access to Juvenile Courts*, Washington, D.C. (periodic); and *Judicial Records*, Washington, D.C. (periodic).

2. Model Policy on Public Access to Court Records, available at www.ncsconline.org, 2002. See "Proposed Policy on Court Records Threatens Public Access Rights," RCFP *The News Media and the Law* (Spring 2002): 8–9.

3. Judicial Conference Committee, Report on Privacy and Public Access to Electronic Case Files (26 June 2001); and "Judges to Allow Access to Some Criminal Cases," RCFP, www.rcfp.org (accessed June 2002).

4. See, for example, *US v Ladd*, 218 F 3d 701 (US 7th Cir Ct Appl), 2000 (identities of unindicted coconspirators must be revealed); and *In re Daily News v Teresi*, 265 AD 2d 129 (Sup Ct NY Appl Div), 2000 (although dismissed as moot due to post-trial release of most records, all sealed records must be released in case involving four police officers charged with beating death of Amadou Diallo).

5. *US v Edwards*, US 5th Cir Ct Appl, MD La, 98–165–13-M2, 2000. See S. L. Alexander, "Their Day in Court," SPJ *Quill* (June 2000): 10–13; and S. L. Alexander, "Trials of the Century: *US v Edwin Edwards* 2000," *Louisiana State Bar Association Journal*, 48:4 (December 2000): 290–294.

6. See, for example, "From the Hotline," RCFP *The News Media and the Law* (Winter 2001): 28.

7. Cited by Timothy Murphy, *Managing Notorious Trials* (Williamsburg, Va.: National Center for State Courts, 1992, 1998), 37, 119.

8. See *In re Dow Jones*, 27 Med. L. Rptr 1156 (US Ct App DC Cir), 1997 (no access to ancillary hearings involving Lewinsky).

9. "Media Allowed to Attend Arraignment of Kennedy Nephew," Associated Press via *Washington Post*, 10 March 2000. See also *Ohio ex rel Dispatch Printing v Loudon*, 241 NE 2d 517 (Ohio Sup Ct), 2001 (trial court erred in closing juvenile delinquency proceeding without a hearing).

10. "Judge Apologizes for Closed Proceeding," Associated Press via *Washington Post*, 21 March 2000.

11. Murphy, *Managing Notorious Trials,* note 7, 35.

12. The RCFP's hotline number is 800–336–4243 and its website is www.rcfp.org. See RCFP, "How to Challenge a Gag Order," in *Secret Justice II: Gag Orders* (Spring 2001).

13. *Arkansas Democrat-Gazette v Zimmerman* 341 Ark 771 (Ark Sup Ct), 2000 (gag overturned in case of a juvenile on trial for attempted murder); and *Albuquerque Journal v Jewel*, 130 NM 64 (NM Sup Ct), 2001 (gag overturned in the case of an overweight child taken into state custody when defendant wanted to speak).

14. See "Judge Modifies Gag Order in Ga Crematorium Case," RCFP *The News Media and the Law* (Spring 2002): 16.

15. *In Re Houston Chronicle*, 64 SW 3d 103 (Texas Ct Appl, 14th Dist), 2001.

16. See "Cloaked in Secrecy, Public Rights Suffer in Westerfield Case," *San Diego Union-Tribune*, 12 May 2002, G-2.

17. *US v Brown*, 218 F 3d 415 (US 5th Cir Ct Appl), 2000. See also S. L. Alexander, "A Reality Check on Court/Media Relations," *Judicature* 84:3 (November–December 2000): 146–149.

18. Murphy, *Managing Notorious Trials,* note 7, 2.

19. See, for example, *Oregonian Publishing v US Dist Ct*, 920 F2d 1462 (US 9th Cir Ct Appl), 1990 (access to plea agreement in a drug case, albeit redactions upheld, 19 Med L Rep 1704, 1991); and *In re Request for Transcripts*, 26 Med L Rptr 2013 (Ca 4th Dist Ct Appl), 1998 (grand jury transcripts released when case settled prior to grand jury deliberations).

Chapter Six

Criminal Cases: The Trial

"WHO WOULD PROFIT FROM THIS BIZARRE MURDER? BESIDES TABLOID JOURNALISM, I MEAN."

Most Americans feel they know what goes on in a courtroom during a trial, thanks to movies and books dealing with the judicial process. The best-selling novels of John Grisham and Scott Turow; movies such as *Witness for the Prosecution* and *Anatomy of a Murder*; and television programs, including the fondly remembered *Perry Mason* and *L.A. Law*, have been influential.

However, the advent of cameras in courtrooms allows journalists, particularly television journalists, to present a more realistic portrait of the judicial process: after all, most hearings do not end up with a blurted-out confession as usually happened when Perry was representing a criminal defendant. Since most Americans are regular television viewers, it is crucial that those responsible for courtroom coverage themselves understand what is occurring in the courtroom. This applies to broadcasters showing courts "live" as well as print journalists writing more in-depth follow-ups.

It is useful, first, to understand the roles of the participants in the process. A detailed look at each stage of the criminal trial process will then be presented, including detailed suggestions for improved coverage.

WHO'S WHO IN THE COURTROOM

The Judge

The judge is the most important person in the courtroom, a fact that those who enter the courtroom would do well to remember at all times. The judge is charged with assuring a defendant in a criminal case a fair trial (and assuring the litigants in a civil case likewise). In a bench trial, the judge determines the facts. In a jury trial, the jury determines the facts while the judge rules on points of law dealing with trial procedure and applies the law. Judges sign warrants and determine bail. They are responsible for scheduling procedures and moving cases along.

Today federal judges are appointed, while as many as 90 percent of state judges are elected, although some are nominated to run for election by state officials or face only re-election votes. For the journalist, this means state judges are sensitive to public opinion of their abilities, and many judges are wary of the press, particularly of courtroom cameras that may broadcast every detail of their conduct in a trial for all to evaluate. However, federal judges are sensitive also, as evidenced by the uproar in 2000 when the US Judicial Conference allowed the release for publication of federal judges' financial records to settle a suit filed in federal district court in New York City by APBNews.com, the (now-defunct) crime and court news website.[1]

The journalist should become familiar with the ABA Code of Judicial Conduct which, as mentioned earlier, although not actually law, is generally expected to be adhered to by judges at all levels of courts. For instance, the extent of a judicial candidate's freedom of speech is controversial, and several have been investigated by judicial commissions for statements made while running for elections.[2] The American Judicature Society has also issued guidelines for judicial candidates.[3] And in 2002, the US Supreme Court heard a Minnesota Republican Party case challenging restrictions on the speech of judicial candidates and held that a rule prohibiting judicial candidates from announcing their views on disputed political and legal issues violated the First Amendment. However, other restrictions, such as a ban on campaign promises by judicial candidates, were not affected by the decision.[4]

Sitting judges have also been criticized. As mentioned in chapter 1, the presiding judge in the Microsoft antitrust case was banned by the appeal court from hearing the retrial on grounds he had presented an appearance of partiality by talking to reporters prior to issuing his decision. A superior court judge in California was censured for explaining to the press some unique sentences he had imposed on defendants in his courtroom.[5] A New York judge was censured for commenting first on the Simpson case and later about a proceeding in his court, one that involved a Bronx school board member.[6]

The judicial canons require judges to follow strict procedures to assure due process rights are upheld. Canon 3A(7) regarding courtroom cameras has already been discussed. Judges also must follow canons requiring them to avoid all appearance of bias, even to the extent of banning of judges' commenting on controversial issues or of telling certain types of jokes. (See appendix B for Code of Judicial Conduct.)

In 1999, the Special Committee of the American Bar Association released a Model Response for Criticism of Judges and Courts that urged bar associations to respond to unjust attacks on judges, especially when a specific pending case is involved or when the attack might affect the course of justice.[7]

The aforementioned judges' handbook *Managing Notorious Trials* repeatedly warns judges to beware the press: "Television, interviews, requests for seats, social approaches—these are intense and persistent. To give in once is to put the judge in a position that he must continue. He must not speak except in court."[8]

As discussed earlier, a trial judge has broad powers to cite for contempt. Judge Ito issued to several reporters covering the Simpson case subpoenas threatening contempt. One of the most widely publicized recent contempt convictions involved Vanessa Leggett, an author writing a book about a murder case in Texas. Leggett refused to reveal a source and was jailed for a record 168 days for contempt,[9] and the US Supreme Court refused to hear her appeal.[10] However, in another case, the Mississippi Supreme Court overturned a contempt finding against a reporter who wrote about a juvenile's court record despite a judge's order not to. The court held the order was an unconstitutional prior restraint.[11]

As a journalist, you should always address a judge with the utmost respect. "Your Honor" or "The Court" are proper terms of address when speaking to a judge.
You must never forget the extent of a judge's contempt power. One Florida

trial judge, particularly testy after two mistrials, was heard to announce in a courtroom that if anyone put anything in his mouth—even a cough drop—he would be cited for contempt.

*You should make a special effort to show the judge how much you prize accuracy. Be on time for all proceedings. Keep up with calendars. Research the records ahead of time. Spell names correctly. Double check dates and statistics.

*Remember: there is no such thing as showing too much respect to a judge! One judge sued a reporter for libel for pointing out (among other things) that the judge often referred to a crystal ball in his courtroom that he consulted for help in decisions.

See chapter 10 for working journalists' specific tips on dealing with judges.

Lawyers

Sometimes nonlawyers forget that lawyers are also officers of the court. As with judges, lawyers are sworn to uphold the rights of all citizens to receive justice from the judicial system; lawyers are also bound by their own rules of conduct, which, like those of the judges, have the effect of law. For instance, although lawyers may discuss the role of the judge and general workings of the court, they may not comment at will on pending cases or describe their strategy in a case.

The rules for lawyers include the ABA Model Rules of Professional Conduct (adopted by more than thirty states) and the ABA Standards for Criminal Justice: Fair Trial and Free Press, adopted by at least forty states. When first passed in 1968, after a series of convictions that were overturned because of due process violations relating to media coverage (see, for example, *Sheppard* and *Estes* described in chapter 2), the standards were very restrictive. A relaxed revision of the standards passed in 1979, while the 1994 revision was an attempt to balance free press and fair trial interests.

Standard 8.1 of the ABA Standards for Criminal Justice, for instance, deals with extrajudicial statements by lawyers, an area of great controversy. Lawyers are forbidden to make statements that would have a "substantial likelihood of prejudicing a criminal proceeding." Specific examples of matters that a lawyer is forbidden to discuss include descriptions of a defendant's character (including possible prior criminal record); his opinion regarding the defendant's guilt; the contents of any possible confession given by the accused; the nature of any physical evidence (including results of exams such as lie detector tests); information regarding possible witnesses; and whether the accused will likely plead guilty to the original charges—in short, anything that the lawyer knows might not be considered admissible evidence during the trial or that would be considered in any way prejudicial. (See appendix B.)

On the other hand, lawyers are specifically allowed to describe the general nature of the charges and the defense; "directory information" such as the name, age, residence, occupation, and family status of the defendant; information necessary to warn the public of any possible danger; a request for help in obtaining evidence in the case; the status of the investigation into the charges; the identity of a victim in a case (if that is not prohibited by law, as in some sexual assaults); any information available as a public record; and the scheduling of the stages of the trial.

In 1991, in *Gentile v State Bar of Nevada*, the US Supreme Court heard an appeal from a lawyer in Nevada challenging these rules. The Court held that lawyers have First Amendment rights of speech, and some restrictions may be too vague to withstand a challenge, but it generally upheld the rules.[12] As a result, in 1994, the ABA revised its restrictive Section 3.6 of the Model Rules of Professional Conduct to allow more leeway for lawyers dealing with the media and to lessen the chance of facing disciplinary proceedings, particularly when a lawyer is responding to out-of-court public comments by the lawyer for the opposing side, the "fair reply" provision. (See appendix B.) More recent challenges to rules restricting lawyers' speech have generally been unsuccessful,[13] although some courts have upheld lawyers' speech rights.[14]

These changes reflect the realization that today members of both the prosecution and defense bars recognize the importance of public opinion in trying a high-profile criminal case—as well as the difficulty of enforcing restrictions regarding lawyer's speech. For instance, in the 1992 William Kennedy Smith rape case, the prosecutor filed a motion to be allowed to introduce evidence of prior sexual harassment incidents, which allowed her to comment for the press on material that (as expected) was ruled inadmissible for use in the trial itself.

In the summer of 1994 in California, the district attorney in the OJ Simpson murder case speculated Simpson would plead guilty as part of an insanity plea; a few days later a defense attorney suggested a racist police officer planted evidence. In 1998, an assistant US attorney prosecuting a kickback scheme involving the New Jersey lottery was sanctioned for releasing documents to the press.[15]

In 1997, New York's high court chief judge, the Hon. Judith Kaye, announced adoption of a new set of voluntary rules governing the conduct of lawyers, at least in that trendsetting state. The "Standards of Civility" call for lawyers to avoid disparaging personal remarks about other lawyers; to refrain from tricks such as pretending a settlement is imminent when there is no real intent to settle; and to acknowledge clients' rights, such as prompt return of phone calls.[16]

In 1998, two law professors were among those who proposed a special code of ethics for lawyers who are not connected with a particular case but merely acting as sources for the press or especially as TV commentators in a highly publicized case.[17] And the same year a professor conducted a fifty-state analysis of trial publicity rules and concluded there is a need to reconsider the broad range of existing state practices and to develop a universal rule consistent with Constitutional principles.[18]

At the same time, there is a growing trend toward "litigation public relations," with lawyers taking a proactive role in "spin control" regarding publicity. For instance, a defense lawyer for OJ Simpson, Robert Shapiro, is one of dozens who have written on the topic "Manipulating the Media."[19] (A full discussion of such writings, along with detailed counter-suggestions, is the subject of chapter 10).

A lawyer may be willing to talk to you "off the record," helping you with background material on a case, when his ethics do not allow him to make public comments. You might do well to establish a relationship with a lawyer prior to the start of a trial.

However, you should remain wary at all times of a lawyer's motivations in "leaking" information to the press. Lawyers are sworn advocates of only one party in a case, and even the best lawyers today admit manipulating the media is an important tactic.

If you need more information than a lawyer handling the case is able to provide, consider contacting a lawyer uninvolved with the case to help you with background information. The local bar association can recommend someone.

Many trial lawyers express the same pet peeves with the media, as do lawyers who have been elevated to the status of judges. Prepare before you interview a lawyer. Explain how limited your "air time" will be if you are a broadcaster. Do not ask a lawyer whose client is on trial whether the client has pleaded Guilty. Do not ask a lawyer to characterize the testimony of a witness. Do not characterize every step of the trial in terms of "win/lose." Do not describe proceedings as the result of a legal "technicality." Try to avoid telling lawyer jokes. (Although you may find lawyers eager to share their favorites with you: do not laugh too loudly!)

Jurors

Much of the concern regarding press coverage of trials focuses, appropriately, on the jurors—and, prior to jury selection, on the effects of possibly prejudicial pre-trial publicity on the Sixth Amendment right of the defendant to a trial by an impartial jury. The journalist needs to recognize that the potential jurors must be dealt with carefully. The judges' and lawyers' codes of conduct require all officers of the court to counteract the effects of pre-trial publicity with detailed questions during jury selection, and in order to avoid "contaminating" fellow members of the *venire,* the potential juror who says he has heard or watched or read possibly prejudicial coverage of the case may be questioned *in camera.*

If it appears the coverage in the locality where the crime occurred is particularly intense, as discussed earlier, a judge is expected to honor requests for remedies such as changing the venue (location) of the trial, changing the *venire* (jury pool) by importing potential jurors from another jurisdiction within the state, or continuing (delaying) the trial until the publicity has died down. Of course, lawyers for both sides will attempt to eliminate any prejudiced jurors from the case (at least those prejudiced against them), but sometimes jurors are not completely candid during *voir dire,* particularly with the growing practice of some tabloid media's encouraging jurors to exploit jury service with post-trial remuneration for interviews and publicity rights.

Another controversial topic today involves juror privacy. In more and more cases, access to jurors' names is kept private, even after the trial. As mentioned in chapter 1, the jurors in the Oklahoma City bombing case were kept behind a screen throughout the trial, obscuring them from the view of closed-circuit TV cameras, and the names of jurors in the 1997 Unabomber case, settled with a plea bargain, were among the records sealed.[20] The press was denied access to *voir dire* proceedings until after the jury was impaneled in the wire fraud trial of boxing promoter Don King.[21] At the trial of a woman charged with extortion of Bill Cosby, the sealing of a transcript of a closed hearing regarding the dismissal of a juror was upheld.[22]

Juror secrecy has become an issue of growing concern. In a 1997 corruption case dealing with the involvement of Louisiana politicians with video poker, the court upheld a ban on even post-verdict interviews: the judge's order was interpreted to deal only with discussion of jury deliberations.[23] The Fifth Circuit has also upheld use of anonymous juries before, during, and after trial in the cases against former Louisiana Governor Edwin Edwards and Insurance Commissioner Jim Brown, despite motions to obtain juror information.[24] And in 2002, reporters were charged with contempt for violating orders not to contact jurors even after a mistrial was declared in the case of a rabbi accused of murdering his wife.[25]

However, in a noted 1998 case involving the trial of former US Senator John Symington, an appeal court held that closed hearings held during jury deliberations, which had been ordered closed without a hearing, were an error by the trial judge.[26] In 2001, the Kentucky Supreme Court held that due to an improper ban on juror access in a murder case, the trial court was to send letters to jurors requiring them to make affirmative requests to continue the ban on post-verdict interviews.[27]

Moreover, the judges' handbook *Managing Notorious Trials* reminds judges that juror anonymity becomes less of an issue after a trial, and judges should address this matter before dismissing jurors: "In all cases, jurors should be told that they may choose to talk to the media if they wish, but the decision is entirely theirs."[28]

As a journalist, you should scrupulously avoid any contact with members of the venire *and those selected to serve on a jury until after the verdict (and if the jury is to recommend a sentence, the sentence recommendation) is announced. Failure to follow this advice can lead to dire consequences. In 1993, for instance, a student intern at one newspaper was cited for contempt for attempting to contact a juror at home, and several worst-case scenarios—in which judges were forced to call mistrials due to a journalist's unethical contact with jurors—have been reported.*
However, as with closed proceedings, if you are covering a case and the court limits all access to jurors, you would want to discuss with your supervisor the possibility of asking your lawyers to file access motions.

Witnesses

News coverage of witnesses is also fraught with peril for the journalist. In many criminal cases, for instance, the court specifically requires witnesses to remain outside the courtroom until their testimony is required. A journalist might interfere with the judicial process by interviewing a witness prior to his testifying and providing the witness with information from the trial that "contaminates" his testimony.

In some cases, journalists themselves are included on the witness list and thus subject to separation orders requiring them to remain outside the courtroom until called.

You should never forget the sensitivities of witnesses personally involved in a case, such as families and friends of crime victims. Treat these people— particularly victims—with the respect you would want granted to you and your loved ones.

Other Court Personnel and the General Public

Both civil and criminal trials require the presence of several court employees throughout the trial. For instance, the **clerk of court**, in addition to performing the pre-trial record-keeping discussed earlier, is responsible for administering the oath to witnesses, handling evidence and exhibits, and generally serving as the judge's assistant throughout the trial.

Next to the lawyers, the court clerk may be the most important contact you might want to cultivate in covering a trial. The clerk can provide you with calendar information; access to documents; names, addresses, and phone numbers of court participants; and valuable tips for coverage.

Similarly, the **court reporter** is an official representative of the court while serving at a trial. He is responsible for the transcripts of the proceedings, the only official record of the case.

Everyone is familiar with the role of the **bailiff**—to maintain order by serving as the judge's law enforcement officer throughout the trial. The bailiff is generally a sheriff's deputy and is an officer of the court. His duties often include arranging seating for the public and press at a trial and taking charge of the jury throughout the trial and especially during deliberations.

A bailiff is another good friend to have in the courtroom. He will monitor your behavior in the courtroom, including where you may sit and when you may enter and leave.

Other law enforcement officials may be involved in the case. These include those who handle evidence, arresting officers, and detectives, as well as guards of defendants who are already in custody. There are some general restrictions on public comments of law enforcement personnel.

In some jurisdictions, a representative of the court system may be available to help the public and the press. The job title might be "public information officer" or "representative of the office of administration." These are knowledgeable, helpful people, selected because of their temperament and willingness to work with the public. Some jurisdictions, such as those in Florida, Louisiana, Minnesota, and New Jersey, seem particularly concerned with selecting qualified personnel.

Also, some jurisdictions in recent years have begun to employ **victim advocates**—either paid or (more often) voluntary participants who are dedicated to smoothing the way for the victim and his family and friends in a criminal trial. Often the victim advocate will regard the press with animosity and attempt to protect the families from press coverage.

Members of the general public will usually be present, particularly at high-profile criminal trials. Colleagues of lawyers trying cases, those with upcoming cases before the same judge, and family and friends of litigants often make for crowded courtrooms.

Litigants

The position of the state in a criminal case is presented to the public by the prosecutor, while that of the defendant is handled by the defense lawyer. A journalist would typically have little access to a defendant before or during a criminal trial—if the defendant is free on bond, his lawyer will likely advise him to avoid all contact with anyone outside the courtroom, and if he is in jail awaiting trial, the journalist would routinely be denied access. The effective and appropriate way to contact the litigants outside the courtroom is through their lawyers. (See Figure 6.1: Who's Who in the Courtroom.)

TRIAL PROCEDURE

After all the pre-trial activity is complete, the trial begins. Jury selection may take anywhere from a few hours to several weeks in a high-profile case, with a journalist often expected to provide a story each day regardless of whether any substantial activity beyond typical *voir dire* takes place.

Remember to translate legal jargon into everyday language. The point of your work is to share your understanding of the proceedings with your audience.
Briefly summarize past developments in each story: most viewers and readers will not have followed proceedings as closely as you. End with a preview of the next step in the trial.
Pay close attention to the questions asked during voir dire, *as they will provide strong clues as to the approach the lawyers will take in trying the case.*

One of the most crucial stages of the trial from the journalist's point of view is the opening statement of each lawyer after the jury is sworn in. The prosecution may present in great detail an outline of the state's case, possibly naming the witnesses in the order in which they will testify and summing up the general nature of the testimony. The defense may similarly outline its case or may delay its opening statement until the second half of the case or (rarely) present no opening statement. It must be remembered opening statements are not evidence.

Often the first few witnesses in a criminal case will be law enforcement officers and others attempting to support the charges by reporting in detail

Figure 6.1

Who's Who in the Courtroom

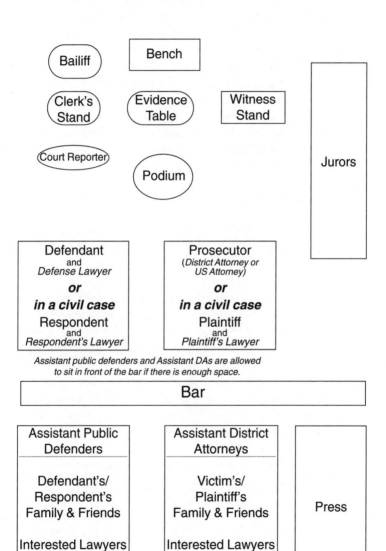

Bailiff

Bench

Clerk's Stand

Evidence Table

Witness Stand

Court Reporter

Podium

Jurors

Defendant
and
Defense Lawyer

or

in a civil case

Respondent
and
Respondent's Lawyer

Prosecutor
(*District Attorney or US Attorney*)

or

in a civil case

Plaintiff
and
Plaintiff's Lawyer

*Assistant public defenders and Assistant DAs are allowed
to sit in front of the bar if there is enough space.*

Bar

Assistant Public Defenders

Defendant's/
Respondent's
Family & Friends

Interested Lawyers

General Public

Assistant District Attorneys

Victim's/
Plaintiff's
Family & Friends

Interested Lawyers

General Public

Press

their activities in connection with the crime, such as the "chain of evidence," that is, the manner in which physical evidence was obtained and preserved. During the cross examination, the typical defense lawyer will attempt to find errors in the process—such as a difference in the descriptions offered by a witness in a statement made immediately after the activity and sworn to in a deposition and the statements made in court, often a year or more later. This attempt to impeach a witness is routinely made and sometimes successful.

One common complaint of lawyers is that journalists, particularly broadcasters, often arrive at a trial unprepared with background knowledge of the case and instead rely on the lawyers to describe all the events of the day for the journalist during a recess. The lawyers are preoccupied with the business at hand, representing their clients, and have no time to do the journalist's work for him. Moreover, the journalist is doing a disservice to the audience by allowing a lawyer to say anything he wants regarding progress on the case, putting his own "spin" on events.

*As advised earlier, you should have fully prepared for the trial, read the file on the case, and established rapport with the major participants ahead of time.
*When you are attempting to interview lawyers during a trial, show courtesy by waiting until they are finished discussing business with their colleagues or clients during a recess and then schedule an interview for a later time.
*Never allow a lawyer simply to describe his version of events without an educated (and nonhostile) questioning of his interpretation. Do not assume interviews with the opposing lawyer will balance your coverage—often one side is not effective or is reluctant to be interviewed during a trial.
*Take a cue from the lawyers: try not to ask one of them a question (particularly if you are a broadcast journalist going "live") to which you do not already have a good idea of what the answer will be.

As mentioned in chapter 3, rules on access to evidence are not universal, and often such rules are not clearly defined by the courts. Generally a reporter has access to evidence that has been filed with the clerk. However, courts are divided on whether there is a right to copy exhibits and evidence used in trials. For instance, a Pennsylvania court supported post-trial access to a videotaped confession of a convicted murderer,[29] and the Virginia Supreme Court ruled that audiotapes of a criminal trial are themselves public record and must be made available to the press and public.[30] In a trial involving charges of police misconduct, a New Jersey court ordered the police department to release the 911 audiotapes used in evidence.[31]

However, in a noted case involving the death of race-car driver Dale Earnhardt, the courts upheld denying access to autopsy photos.[32] Moreover, Florida legislators passed a retroactive law providing for confidentiality of photographs and video and audio records of autopsies,[33] and the law, repeatedly challenged, became a model for several other states.

The case files themselves are usually available to the public to view before and after the trial in the clerk's office. During the trial a copy of the file may remain in the clerk's office or may be available in the office of the presiding judge.

By the time the trial begins, the file in a criminal case should include the following: the information sheet, the complaint, the indictment or information, affidavits of arresting officers, warrants and returns, documents relating to bail, and records of any pre-trial proceedings such as discovery material or preliminary hearings. By the end of the trial, the file would also include jury lists, jury instructions, verdict forms, and, eventually, judgments and sentences.

After the prosecution has presented its witnesses, the prosecutor will announce the government has rested its case. At this time, as discussed earlier, the defense will routinely file several motions, including moving the judge to direct a verdict of acquittal due to the state's failure to present enough evidence to meet the burden of proof. Such motions should be noted in the journalist's report, although they are rarely granted.

The public generally finds defense witnesses of great interest in a criminal trial. Many of the cases that survive the judicial process until the trial stage involve heinous crimes such as murder. Most interesting of all in many such cases is the defendant himself.

Remember, despite the realities described earlier, legally a defendant is presumed innocent until proven guilty; he is not required to present any witnesses or to testify on his own behalf. Do not speculate that his failure to testify casts any doubt on the defendant's innocence.

At the conclusion of testimony, when the defense rests its case, once again the lawyers will make motions that should be noted. Then, when the judge reads the instructions to the jury, he may lock the courtroom to keep distractions to a minimum. The instructions are hard-fought guidelines for the jury to follow and often are a crucial element in conviction or acquittal and may be cited in an appeal.

Resist the temptation to leave the courtroom during the reading of the jury instructions. Note any crucial elements for use in your report on the verdict.

If you must leave the courthouse during deliberations, be sure you have a fail-safe contact to let you know when to return for the verdict.

The most dramatic portion of any criminal trial generally is the announcement of the verdict by the judge, jury foreman, or clerk. The deliberations may have taken less than an hour or several days, and the length of the deliberations should be noted in the journalist's report, along with the exact charges, the date of the sentencing, and the reactions of key participants— defendants, lawyers, witnesses, victims, and families.

If you are interviewing participants in a criminal trial after a verdict is announced, do not forget to consider the emotional states of all those personally involved. Do not ask anyone, "How do you feel?" A victim or family member or friend will have an emotional reaction to the verdict, as will the defendant's loved ones, particularly if the defendant is convicted.

The work of the journalist is not completed when the verdict is announced. Specific suggestions for coverage of post-trial activity including sentencing and appeals are the subject of chapter 7.

NOTES

1. *APBNews.com v Committee on Financial Disclosure*, filed 1999 (settled). Cited in "Judges Decide to Release Financial Disclosure Forms to News Service," RCFP *The News Media and the Law* (Spring 2000): 7–8.

2. See, for example, *Pittman v Cole*, 267 F 3d 1269, (US 11th Cir Ct Appl), 2001 (question of sanctions for Alabama judges who answered Christian Coalition questionnaire was remanded to state Supreme Court).

3. Cynthia Gray, *Communicating With Voters: Ethics and Judicial Campaign Speech* (Chicago: American Judicature Society, 2000).

4. *Republican Party of Minnesota v White*, 122 S Ct 2528 (2002).

5. *Broadman v Commission on Judicial Performance*, 18 Cal 4th 1079 (Ca Sup Ct), 1998.

6. *In re Douglas McKeon*, cited in "Actions Taken against Judges for Talking to Media Contested," *The News Media and the Law* (Fall 1998): 16–17.

7. A. P. Carlton, "ABA Strives to Save a Constitutional Impartial Judiciary," *(Sacramento, Calif.) Daily Recorder*, 20 September 1999.

8. Timothy Murphy, *Managing Notorious Trials* (Williamsburg, Va.: National Center for State Courts, 1992, 1998), 7.

9. See, for example, Robert Buckman, "'I Feel Stronger,'" SPJ *Quill* (January/February 2002): 18–22.

10. *Leggett v US, In re Grand Jury Subpoenas*, US Ct App 5th Cir (unpublished) No 01–20745, 29 Med L Rptr 2301, 2001, *cert den*, 122 S Ct 1593 (2002).

11. *Jeffries v Mississippi*, 724 So 2d 897 (Miss Sup Ct) 1998.

12. *Gentile v State Bar of Nevada*, 501 US 1030 (1991).

13. See, for example, *Devine v Robinson*, 131 F Supp 2d 963 (US Dist Ct N Dist Ill), 2001 (Illinois Supreme Court dismissed action challenging ban on lawyers' extrajudicial statements).

14. See, for example, *US v Scarfo* 263 F 3rd 80 (US 3d Cir Ct Appl), 2001 (former lawyer's comments would not have prejudicial effect on case).

15. *US v Smith*, 992 F Supp 743 (US Dist Ct NJ), 1998.

16. Gary Spencer, "Tougher Lawyer Sanction Rule Imposed," *New York Law Journal*, 18 September 1997, 1; and Richard Perez-Pena, "New York to Allow Bigger Fines on Lawyers' Nuisance Tactics," *New York Times*, 18 September 1997, B6.

17. Michael Higgins, "Rules to Talk By," *ABA Journal* (February 1998): 20–21.

18. Kathy Fitzpatrick, "Free Speech v Fair Trial," manuscript, AEJMC National Convention, 8 August 1998.

19. Robert Shapiro, "Secrets of a Celebrity Lawyer," *Columbia Journalism Review* (September–October 1994): 25–29.

20. *Unabomb Trial Media Coalition v US Dist Ct*, 183 F 3d 949 (US 9th Cir No. 97–7318), 1999.

21. *In re US v King*, 140 F 3d 76 (US Ct Appl DC Cir), 1998.

22. *US v Jackson*, 969 F Supp 881 (SD NY, 1997).

23. *In re US v Carl Cleveland, et al*, 128 F 3d 267 (US 5th Cir Ct Appl), 1997; and *cert den, In re Capital City Press,* 523 US 1075, 1998.

24. *US v Edwards*, 119 F Supp 2d 589 (US 5th Cir Ct Appl), 2000; and *US v Brown*, 250 F 3d 907 (US 5th Cir Ct Appl), 2001. See also Reporters Committee for Freedom of the Press, *Secret Justice I: Anonymous Juries*, Fall 2000.

25. *New Jersey v Neulander*, 171 NJ 332 (unpublished), 2002 (leave to appeal).

26. *Phoenix News v US Dist Ct,* 156 F 3d 940 (US 9th Cir Ct Appl), 1998.

27. *Cape Publs v Braden*, 39 SW 3d 823 (Ky Sup Ct), 2001.

28. Murphy, *Managing Notorious Trials*, 60.

29. *Commonwealth v Gallman* 48 Pa D & C 4th 413 (Phil Ct Common Pleas), 2001.

30. *Smith v Richmond News*, 261 Va 113 (Va Sup Ct), 2001.

31. See "New Jersey Judge Orders Release of 911 Tapes," Reporters Committee for Freedom of the Press, www.rcfp.org, (accessed April 2002); and *In re Daily Journal v Police*, 797 A 2d 186 (Supr Ct NJ), 2002 (however, records not yet entered into evidence did not have to be released).

32. *Earnhardt v Volusia County*, Fla Cir Ct Volusia Cty, 29 Med L Rptr 2173, 2001.

33. Fla. Stat. Sect. 406.135 Public Health, Medical Examiners: Autopsies; Confidentiality of photographs and video and audio recordings (2001). See, for example, La R S 44:19 Public Records and Recorders: Autopsy photographs, video, and other visual images (2002).

Chapter Seven

Criminal Cases: Post-Trial Activity

"O.K., you've just sentenced him to twenty-five years to life—now push 'send.'"

After the trial is completed, the job of the journalist is not over. Subsequent proceedings include possible sentencing hearings in the case of a criminal conviction and motion hearings, as well as appeals, which may result in re-hearings or remanded re-trials. Upon exhaustion of the appeals process, possible probations and pardons in criminal cases are possible. Follow-through is one of the most neglected areas of coverage of the judicial process.

SENTENCING

After a criminal conviction, a judge will often order a pre-sentencing investigation: this report is generally confidential. Relatives and friends of the convicted will be consulted and may appear at a hearing to testify and to request leniency of the sentencing judge. A controversial area involves the request of supporters of the victim(s) in a criminal case to have a voice at the sentencing hearing. The law is currently in a state of flux regarding what outside considerations a judge is to take into account at the time of sentencing.

As discussed earlier, final sentencing hearings are held in open court. Multiple sentences, it will be remembered, may be served concurrently (simultaneously) or consecutively (one after another). Sentences may be suspended (eliminated) and a defendant may be put on probation, required to meet certain restrictions for a set period of time or to face re-imposition of the sentence.

Note whether any restitution or victim compensation is ordered and include this in your story.
A convicted defendant may be successful in having his sentence reduced at subsequent hearings. A good journalist will keep track of sentence reduction hearings.

APPEALS

Almost any major felony conviction will be followed by an appeal. In some instances such as capital cases, appeals are automatic. Grounds for appeal must include a contention that the verdict was not supported by the evidence or some other suggestion of wrongdoing by the court.

Never ask a defendant's lawyer in a high-profile criminal case whether his client will appeal. Assume he will and ask to see the notice of appeal, the record (prepared by the court reporter), and the briefs of the lawyers arguing each side's case.
Keep track of the appeal as it moves through the system. If there are oral arguments, arrange for coverage.

Intermediate appellate courts, available in federal cases and in about half the states, generally meet in panels of three judges to consider appeals. The decisions are usually handed down in written form. Convictions upheld by intermediate courts may be appealable to the state's highest court or, in federal cases, the US Supreme Court.

Appeals to a high court are taken as writs of *certiorari*: in most cases, just fewer than half the judges must agree to "take the writ" for the case to be considered. The thinking is that if most of the judges agree with the decision as it stands, there is no point in arguing to overturn the lower court's decision.

*If the appeal court does not take the writ, this should be described accurately; it is not the same thing as "upholding" the lower court's decision.

After a defendant has exhausted all appeals in state courts, he may have the right to file a *habeas corpus*, one meaning of which is a petition to **remove** or transfer the case to the federal court. With few exceptions, such appeals are not automatic: the defendant must charge some error of constitutional dimension was made in his trial.

As discussed, few cases appealed to the US Supreme Court actually are accepted by the justices. In recent years, only 100 or so cases out of the 7,000 petitions submitted annually are heard by the High Court. A small portion of these are applications, or requests for emergency action addressed to an individual justice. For instance, applications for stays (delays) of execution make for dramatic news stories.

About two dozen reporters regularly cover the proceedings of the US Supreme Court, including those from a number of large newspapers as well as wire services Associated Press (AP) and Reuters. None of the major television networks has a full-time reporter, nor do the major national news weeklies. There is only enough room at present for about three dozen members of the press corps in the courtroom, so access is controlled by the Public Information Office. Since the 1930s, there has been a pressroom in the court building with a limited number of desks, computer outlets, and phones. Obviously press credentials must be arranged for in advance.

As noted, as of this writing there is no broadcast coverage permitted of Supreme Court proceedings, with the only exception the delayed audiotaping of the 2000 *Bush-Gore* election case. In fact, the justices are so camera-shy that there is only one known photograph of the Court in session, taken surreptitiously in 1935.[1]

In 2000, the US Supreme Court instituted a useful website (supremecourt us.gov). Included are biographies of present and past justices, the docket, oral argument transcripts and briefs, opinions, media advisories regarding high-profile cases, press releases, and an in-depth reporter's guide to applications.[2] The site also includes links to other government sites of interest such as the Administrative Office of the US Courts (www.uscourt.gov); the Federal Judicial Center (www.fjc.gov), which is the education and research agency for federal courts; the US Sentencing Commission (www.ussc.gov), and the National Association of State Sentencing Commissions (www.ussc.gov/states).

The Supreme Court also provides helpful information via telephone. The Public Information Office is at 202–479–3211, and Opinion Announcements are at 202–479–3360. The public information officer as of this writing is Kathleen Arberg.

In addition to private databases mentioned earlier such as FindLaw and Court TV (both free) and Lexis One and West Doc (free/fee), as of this writing there are several other useful sites for covering federal appeals courts. Emory University Law School's "Federal Courts Finder" (http://law.emory .edu/FEDCTS) includes federal appeal courts, and both Cornell University Law School (http://supct.law.cornell.edu) and Northwestern University Law School's "On the Docket" (http://medill.northwestern.edu/docket) include opinions and informative background stories on recent and upcoming US Supreme Court cases. Since 1999, the *New York Times* home page (www. nytimes.com), under "Politics," has posted court information, including an online question-and-answer column by the paper's Pulitzer Prize–winning Supreme Court correspondent, Linda Greenhouse.

During the session of the US Supreme Court, holdings are usually announced Mondays from October through June. Check for descriptions of upcoming cases of interest in your area.
Local lawyers and law professors can help interpret High Court cases for you. Try to find an objective party to put the decision in perspective.

Several commentators have criticized press coverage of the High Court. For instance, authors of a full-length book on television coverage of the Court were highly critical of the failure of television networks adequately to cover the Court: the study showed each year fewer and fewer stories were covered, and those that were aired were often faulty.[3] A 1999 article in *Brill's Content* said the Supreme Court reporters may be "Washington's most deferential press corps" and also said the press was "falling down in its role as a watchdog for an entire branch of government."[4]

Professor Dru Riley Evarts completed a project in which she sat through an entire session of the Court. According to Evarts, who spoke to all of the regular members of the press corps, journalists generally lunched together during the session, often joined by the court public information officer and sometimes the clerk of court.

Evarts gathered suggestions to help journalists improve coverage. For instance, although tapes of High Court's arguments were available immediately and transcribed ten days later, respondents said they need to be more complete, including making clear which justice is speaking. Respondents to her survey also requested explanations of the justices' reasoning in individual cases, the justices' reasons for refusing to review cases, and the televising of oral arguments.[5]

Of course, very few cases end up in the US Supreme Court. Sometimes after an appeal has failed, new evidence might surface, and the defendant might move for a new trial. Or on those rare occasions when an appellate court overturns a lower court decision, the case may be reversed and remanded—sent back to the trial court for another trial.

When a re-trial occurs, the work of the journalist begins anew. These cases call for particular caution in order to avoid prejudicial publicity on the part of the journalist when reporting on an earlier conviction.

Should a conviction stand after all attempts at court appeals are exhausted, a last resort would be for a defendant to move for clemency in the form of a **pardon**. A pardon may be a **commutation** (reduction) of a sentence or a full pardon (elimination of the sentence). Pardons are generally issued by the president in a federal case or the governor in a state case. Similarly, a **parole** may be granted, which suspends a sentence after it has been partially served. Finally, carrying out of the ultimate punishment—the death penalty—may be **stayed** (halted temporarily) while a petition for a pardon is pending. Many prisoners in the US spend years on death row, awaiting the exhaustion of the full range of legal alternatives available, before the sentence is carried out.

As discussed earlier, in general civil procedure is similar to criminal procedure. Specific suggestions for covering civil cases—similar to those discussed in the last three chapters for criminal cases—are described in chapter 8.

NOTES

1. Steve France, "Supreme Court Report: A Penchant for Privacy," *ABA Journal* (December 1998): 38.

2. U.S. Supreme Court Public Information Office, "A Reporter's Guide to Applications Pending Before the Supreme Court of the United States," www.supremecourtus.gov (accessed May 2002).

3. Eliot Slotnick and Jennifer Segal, *Television News and the Supreme Court* (New York: Cambridge University Press, 1998).

4. Robert Schmidt, "May It Please the Court," *Brill's Content* (October 1999): 73.

5. Dru Riley Evarts, "A Survey of the US Supreme Court Press Corps," manuscript, AEJMC National Convention, 8 August 1998.

Chapter Eight

Civil Cases

"CUT! CUT! I MEAN ORDER! ORDER!"

When most members of the public think of trials, they think of criminal trials. However, in general, the majority of cases heard in state courts are civil cases. Coverage of civil actions remains one of the areas most neglected by journalists today.

It is often forgotten that the writers of the US Constitution recognized the importance of civil suits. The Seventh Amendment guarantees the right to a jury trial in all civil actions involving 20 dollars or more.

Civil cases often deal with important issues that make good subjects for journalistic scrutiny. Such topics would include abortion, affirmative action, antitrust, bankruptcy, civil rights, copyright, domestic law (divorces and child custody including custody disputes involving surrogate parents), insurance (accidents and personal injury, natural disasters, health and illness), libel, intentional infliction of emotional distress and invasion of privacy, patent and trademark disputes, prison overcrowding, product liability, real estate and property, right-to-die, school prayer, sexual harassment, small claims disputes (the public was fascinated with the televised *People's Court*), taxes, and wills and distribution of estates ("probate"). The federal government itself brings cases such as those involving banking, challenges to the president, and national security issues.

Journalists looking for ideas for civil case coverage might start with legal publications found in law libraries and all or at least in part online. Good sources include the monthly *American Lawyer* (www.americanlawyer.com), the weekly *National Law Journal* (www.nlj.com), and the daily *Legal Times* (www.legaltimes.com), all available via American Lawyer Media's online Law.com (www.law.com). *Lawyers Weekly* (www.lawyersweekly.com) is useful, as is the monthly *American Bar Association Journal* (www.abajour nal.com), which often includes previews of litigation.

American Lawyer Media also maintains information on all fifty states, with in-depth coverage, as of this writing, of eight states. And as mentioned previously, information on cases is available via online databases such as Lexis, Westlaw, Court TV, and government sites. The Judicial Conference, it will be remembered, voted in 2001 to open many civil records to online access.

Particularly newsworthy cases would include **class action** suits. Unlike the criminal case, in which the proceedings are confined to matters concerning the defendant(s) charged, a civil case might be one in which the plaintiffs' lawyer files on behalf of a large group or class of people who would be affected by the result, as in the 1994 *Domestic Air Transportation Antitrust Litigation*,[1] an airline rate case in which more than four million people received remuneration due to the airlines' misconduct. Subsequent high-profile class action cases involved the tobacco and tire industries. Securities class action case information may be found at the Stanford University Law School's "Security Class Action Clearinghouse," (http://securities.stanford.edu). General case information may be found at the National Archives and Records Administration, NARA (www.gpo.gov/nara/index).

Lawyer/reporter Peter Levin, while media administrator for federal courtroom cameras in Pennsylvania, encouraged broadcast stations in his area to cover more civil actions.[2] Some cases covered in his state included a sixty-three-year-old woman's age discrimination case, a stockbroker's suit against a cigarette manufacturer for a cancer he claimed developed due to the asbestos formerly used in the cigarette filters, and a US Senator's suit against the Navy for closing a local shipyard (in all of these, the plaintiffs lost). Other civil cases included that of a pregnant female pathologist who sued a hospital for requiring her to perform autopsies on infants, a DJ who filed suit after losing her job after returning to work from maternity leave, and a hotel guest's suit after he was beaten and evicted because of a mix-up over a previous unpaid bill.

It is true many cases filed in civil courts seem petty or silly. The court system punishes lawyers with fines and other sanctions if they consistently file cases that are patently frivolous or, even worse, filed maliciously, and such sanctions are themselves legitimate findings on which to base news stories.

As discussed in chapter 4, the trial in a civil action follows a process similar to that of a criminal case. As mentioned earlier, some of the terminology differs slightly. For instance, instead of the state prosecuting a defendant, a plaintiff sues a defendant (also called a "respondent"). Rather than being "convicted," a defendant is found "liable."

Moreover, some of the details of the process differ. For example, when researching a civil action, a journalist might find the records are filed by name as in a criminal case or categorized by type of case: labor, contracts, or property. In addition to the type of pre-trial motions filed in criminal cases, civil actions often include voluminous requests for discovery material and frequently requests for summary judgments. After a trial, unlike a criminal case where the state cannot appeal an acquittal, either litigant in most civil cases may attempt an appeal. Also, a common result of an appeal court in a civil action is a **mandamus**, in which a court orders a lower court to take some action.

From the journalist's point of view, a major difference in civil cases compared with criminal cases is that the desire of many civil litigants for privacy may preclude access to part or even all of the proceedings. For instance, depositions and other pre-trial records of witnesses' testimony may not be public; in most jurisdictions, a deposition does not become public until it is formally **filed** with the court. The only US Supreme Court case involving access to such records was a unique case in which the press itself was a litigant: back in 1984, the Court found that the First Amendment did not compel access to unfiled discovery material.[3] This has been an area of much controversy in recent years, with some journalists successfully winning access to depositions, such as those made by Microsoft's Bill Gates, as mentioned in chapter 1.

Journalists also may resort to motions to intervene in order to obtain access to other documents and proceedings. For instance, in a 2001 case involving R. J. Reynolds Tobacco, the media sued to have a gag lifted: the court held that the issue was moot because the case had been settled out of court.[4] In one of several cases against tire manufacturer Bridgestone/Firestone, also settled before trial, after press motions the trial court unsealed some records and was ordered by the appeal court to decide whether "good cause" such as trade secrets existed to keep others sealed.[5]

Perhaps the biggest civil court records access case to date was the one involving a contract dispute between actor Clint Eastwood and his former companion Sondra Locke, where the California Supreme Court ruled in 1999 that the public has an interest in all civil cases, and thus settlement records should be opened.[6] California subsequently passed new rules prohibiting sealing records in civil cases unless an overriding interest is found.

In a later case involving a settlement of a case where a public college terminated the vice president's employment contract, the records were also ordered released. The court said, "Documents in judicial files are presumptively open to the public, and neither the magistrate judge nor any of the parties has given us any reason to think the presumption might be rebutted in this case."[7]

As can be seen, appellate courts have both supported and overruled the sealing of records in civil cases. In some states, legislation is pending regarding the opening of sealed records when the case involves a matter of public importance.

A contempt case developed when a trial judge punished two reporters for publishing information about a settlement when a court clerk mistakenly gave one of them records meant to be sealed. In North Carolina, residents of a trailer park had sued the energy company Conoco over a contaminated water supply. The appeal court overturned a contempt citation against the reporter who had benefited from the error and a second citation against another reporter at the same paper who had obtained confirmation information but had refused to reveal his source of the settlement terms.[8]

The Reporters Committee for Freedom of the Press (RCFP) has published a list of suggestions for reporters attempting to obtain access to sealed settlements: try to obtain as much background information as possible from lawyers even if actual records are sealed; try other sources such as government (Federal Drug Administration) and private (Better Business Bureau) agencies, family and friends of plaintiffs, and former company employees (if not bound by confidentiality agreements). As a last resort, file motions to obtain documents.[9] As in a criminal case, the Reporters Committee Hotline also offers help: 1–800–336–4243, or www.rcfp.org.

However, in general, covering a civil action is similar to covering a criminal case. The reporter would start with obtaining background information. The case file would include the complaint and answer, motions or stipulations, subpoenas, depositions and interrogatories, records of pre-trial proceedings, and eventually all the trial documents as in a criminal trial.

Peter Levin, who, as mentioned, encourages more coverage of civil actions, offered some specific tips for reporters covering civil cases:

Remember that just as a criminal case is effectively presented with an emphasis on the people involved, a civil case is also a "people" story, so you should try to present a picture of the people behind the issues.
You may feel more free to interview witnesses and trial participants prior to a civil trial than in a criminal trial with its potential threat to due process.
Research the issues involved in a civil case. You can start with the online databases or the legal index at the nearest law library.
Follow up a few months after the trial. What happened to the participants? Are they still doing business as before? Have similar suits been filed since the verdict?[10]

A term frequently encountered by the journalist covering civil courts is **"information and belief"**—by which the plaintiff is saying that although he has no firsthand knowledge on which the claim is based, he has reason to believe that the information might be true.

Thus, the journalist covering civil pleadings should be particularly careful to note that the complaint states mere allegations. The journalist should attribute the claim to the party bringing the complaint and qualify the allegations with appropriate language such as, "The complaint alleges. . . ."

Another major difference in civil cases compared with criminal ones is the possibility the case might be filed on a **contingency** basis, which means the lawyer, rather than collecting a set fee, is to be paid based on the amount of the judgment or settlement. The public may be especially interested in these cases, some of them handled by lawyers who advertise heavily on television and promise large sums of money to plaintiffs.

In fact, the issue of lawyers advertising themselves has been the subject of several court cases such as the landmark *Florida Bar v Went For It*,[11] which upheld Florida restrictions on "ambulance chasing" by requiring lawyers to wait at least thirty days before sending letters of solicitation to victims of accidents or catastrophes. The case inspired the development of similar restrictions in other states and, as with other changes in regulation of the legal profession, is itself a good subject for news coverage.

A consortium of legal associations, the American Board of Trial Advocates (ABOTA), has posted an Accuracy in Legal Journalism Reporting Code on its website (www.abota.org). Suggestions for reporters of civil cases include giving the same amount of coverage to the defense's case as to the plaintiff's case; describing whether the case is a "paper verdict" only (when the defendant has no assets to cover the judgment); and following up the appeals, such as reporting when large verdicts are ultimately reduced.[12]

As mentioned earlier, more and more civil cases are being handled outside the court system, in various methods of alternative dispute resolution. The Reporters Committee for Freedom of the Press studied the issue in 2001 and found that such settlements are often closed unless one of the parties is a public body or unless the parties submitted the settlement to the court for public approval.[13]

In 2002, the American Bar Association approved the Uniform Mediation Act, which may be adopted on a state-by-state basis.[14] The confidentiality section of the act allows the parties to choose whether to keep mediation proceedings and documents sealed from the public. However, the act recognizes that rules in some states require revealing information if someone's safety is at stake and that public records laws in many states require revealing certain information to the public.

Court TV, one of the exceptions to the aforementioned generalization that civil cases are generally underreported by the news media, has televised more than 200 civil cases since its inception. These include the Woody Allen/Mia Farrow child custody hearings, the *Twiggs v Mays* (hospital baby-mix-up-at-birth) custody proceedings, the subway vigilante Bernard Goetz libel suit, Art Buchwald's copyright suit against Paramount Pictures, a General Motors class action case, and a trademark dispute between Avis and Hertz.

Coverage of both civil and criminal cases by Court TV and other news organizations, as well as still photography coverage by print media, is the subject of chapter 9.

NOTES

1. *In re Domestic Air Transportation Antitrust Litigation*, 24 Fed R Serv 3d (Callaghan) 515, (US Dist Ct, MD Ga), 1994.

2. Peter Levin, "You Want Me to Read a What?" *Media Studies Journal* 6:1 (Winter 1992): 173–181.

3. *Seattle Times v Rhinehart*, 467 US 20 (1984).

4. *Dow Jones v Kaye*, 256 F 3d 1251, (US 11th Cir Ct Appl), 2001.

5. *Chicago Tribune v Bridgestone/Firestone*, 263 F 3d 1304 (US 11th Cir Ct Appl), 2001.

6. *NBC (KNBC) v Supr Ct L A*, 20 Cal 4th 1178 (Cal Sup Ct), 1999.

7. *Jessup v Luther*, 277 F 3d 926, 931 (US 7th Cir Ct Appl), 2002. See also *In re*

Memphis Publishing 29 Med L Reptr 2565 (Miss Sup Ct) 2001 (after death of boy's mother was concealed by him for more than a month, court held that although parts of the record involving his custody might be closed, portions involving his estate must be opened); and *Anonymous v Anonymous*, 263 A D 2d 341 (NY Sup Ct Appl) 2000 (child custody and support hearing of NYC Mayor Rudolph Giuliani should be open).

8. *Ashcraft v Conoco*, 218 F 3d 282, 288 (US 4th Cir Ct Appl), 2000. See Mary-Ellen Roy, "First Amendment Protects the Openness of Civil Trials," *IRE Journal* (March–April 2000): 11–13.

9. Ashley Gauthier, "Secret Settlements: Hiding Defects, Hurting the Public," RCFP *The News Media and the Law* (Fall 2000): 4.

10. Levin, "You Want Me to Read a What?" 173–181.

11. *Florida Bar v Went For It*, 515 US 618 (1995).

12. American Board of Trial Advocates, "Accuracy in Legal Journalism Reporting Code," www.abota.org (accessed April 2002).

13. RCFP, *Secret Justice III: Alternative Dispute Resolution* (Fall 2001).

14. *Uniform Mediation Act*, National Conference of Commissioners on Uniform State Laws, 2001, www.nccusl.org (accessed 2002).

Chapter Nine

Cameras in Courtrooms

TRUTH · JUSTICE · MERCY
(AS SEEN ON TV)

Crime is something shameful, and it is highly dangerous to advertise criminals as if they were as interesting as Presidents or Prime Ministers or film stars or professional footballers.

—Honorable Robert Bernays, British MP, 1938

The controversy regarding cameras in courtrooms has been around for more than sixty years. However, recent developments involving cameras in state courts as well as experiments with cameras in federal courts necessitate a fresh look at courtroom cameras, especially by broadcast journalists and news photographers.

DEVELOPMENT OF COURTROOM CAMERAS

As mentioned earlier, as of 2002 all fifty states permit some type of camera coverage, whether on an experimental or permanent basis. Most states allow coverage of both trial and appellate courts, and a few allow coverage of appellate courts only.[1]

Cameras had been banned in federal courts since the 1946 adoption of Rule 53 of the Federal Rules of Criminal Procedure.[2] In 1972, the US Judicial Conference incorporated the ABA Code of Judicial Conduct Canon 3A(7) (see appendix B) and subsequently issued a separate policy statement on courtroom cameras (see appendix C).

However, in 1990, after extensive lobbying by a coalition of media groups, the US Judicial Conference began a three-year experiment with cameras in civil courts, and in 1996 voted to allow the thirteen individual appellate circuits to decide whether cameras should be allowed in federal appeals courts. The conference also voted to discourage cameras in federal district (trial) courts. To date, only the Second and Ninth Circuits have approved coverage within their jurisdictions. More than a dozen of the ninety-four federal trial courts have permitted camera coverage of some (mostly civil) cases.

In 1997, Congress began to consider the Sunshine in the Courtroom Act, a proposal to allow coverage of all federal court proceedings at the discretion of the presiding judge. The legislation became part of the Judicial Reform Act of 1998 and was re-introduced in 2000 and 2001.[3]

In 1994, the Federal Judicial Center released a report that showed that more than 250 cases were covered in federal courts during the first two years of the experiment. Significantly, 83 percent of the respondents reported the cameras had little or no effect on the process of judicial administration.[4]

The results of the survey regarding the federal experiment came as no surprise. Traditional objections to courtroom cameras revolve around their presumed impact on the process of the trial. Some legal scholars have suggested cameras violate the privacy of witnesses and jurors, warp public understanding of courtroom procedures, and are an added burden on the trial judge and on court administrators. However, others suggest a camera ban, if based on distinguishing between print and electronic media, is unconstitutional, and many argue for camera coverage with narrow exceptions.

Some social science research has also been conducted, albeit mostly under experimental settings, to test the apparent effects of courtroom cameras. With few exceptions, the empirical evidence gathered to date fails to support the speculation that cameras interfere with the judicial process.[5]

A significant step was taken in the development of courtroom camera coverage when the Courtroom Television Network (Court TV) signed on in 1991.

Backers of Court TV, which cost more than $60 million to start up, included Time Warner and Cablevision; the network was headed until 1997 by Steven Brill, founding publisher of *American Lawyer*.

By the end of its tenth year of operation, Court TV reached more than 65 million viewers and had covered dozens of federal court proceedings. More than 700 cases had been selected for coverage (of the estimated 2 million each year in the US), including more than 100 civil cases. Highly publicized trials covered gavel-to-gavel included the police brutality trial involving Rodney King, the rape trial of William Kennedy Smith, and the murder trials of the Menendez brothers and of OJ Simpson. Court TV had also begun releasing condensed coverage of cases for home video and supplying coverage of some trials over the Internet.[6]

Court TV conducted a survey of judges who had experience presiding over trials during the first four years of its service and reported that 98 percent found the cameras had no effect on the judicial process in their courtrooms.[7] And after a trial court judge proclaimed a New York ban on courtroom cameras unconstitutional in 2000,[8] Court TV sued to have the ban thrown out.

Thus, with the advent of Court TV, the introduction of cameras into some federal courts, and all states now allowing camera coverage, cameras are becoming a fixture in courtrooms. And Internet coverage—such as the online release of the Starr Report in the Clinton case and then the first batch of Watergate tapes online in 2002—has led to a new concern with other issues such as video teleconferences and the dissemination by a newspaper or broadcast station of trial records obtained from online sources.

Florida began televising oral arguments live by satellite and over the Internet in an experiment beginning in 1997.[9] In 1999, a Florida attempted-murder trial became the first trial netcast in full by a court system live over the Internet.[10]

In 1999, a study for the National Center for State Courts predicted that the "virtual trial," taking place electronically, was still in the future, but that trials already were possible with significant portions conveyed electronically.[11] Videoconferencing, online calendaring, video depositions, video witness testimony, and online trial transcripts are already found in courtrooms throughout the country. For the corruption trial of former Louisiana Governor Edwin Edwards in 2000, docket information was posted online on the court's website; the judge, defendants, lawyers, jurors, and members of the press wore headsets allowing them to listen to the extensive audiotaped evidence; the judge could turn on "white noise" allowing only himself, defendants, and lawyers to hear information; and everyone could view documentary evidence on eight terminals shared by jurors and two shared by the public and the press.

GUIDELINES FOR COURTROOM CAMERAS

The federal government and each state allowing coverage have promulgated guidelines for use of cameras in courts. (See Figure 9.1: Courtroom Camera Guidelines.) The guidelines for use of cameras in federal trial courts during the experimental period (1991–1994) are a useful example for discussion. (See appendix C.)

In adopting the Guidelines for the Pilot Program on Photographing, Recording and Broadcasting in the Courtroom (issued September 12, 1990), the US Judicial Conference followed the same model as that found in most states. The first section of the guidelines spells out the limits of coverage—in this case, the guidelines were valid only for the experimental period and only in selected civil district courts. A handful of states are still in the experimental stage, while most already have adopted permanent rules. Most of the states allowing trial coverage allow coverage of both civil and criminal cases. The federal courts and more than half the states require advance notice to the court, the court's permission before allowing camera coverage, or both. In some states, the consent of the parties involved in the litigation is required for courtroom camera coverage.

*A good journalist would respectfully notify the court as far in advance as possible of the desire to use cameras. And if you are in a state that requires notice or permission, you should make every attempt to meet more than the minimum requirement.
*If you are working in one of these states, allow as much time as possible to obtain parties' consent; hearings may have to be scheduled in advance of the trial.

The first section of the federal guidelines concludes with notice that any expense of courtroom camera coverage must be borne by the media (a common stipulation in many states' guidelines) and a reminder that in order to maintain due process, a judge might add additional restrictions in individual cases.

The second section of the federal guidelines includes a restriction found in most states that there be no audio pickup or broadcast of either bench conferences (between the judge and the lawyers) or of conferences between the lawyers and the client or among the lawyers serving as cocounsel.

*Respect the sanctity of bench conferences and of the attorney-client relationship upon which this guideline is based.

Figure 9.1
Courtroom Camera Guidelines

A=Appellate Courts   B=Background shots only   C=Certain types of cases only   T=Trial Courts   U=Upon arrival of judge; or unless juror objects   N=No   Y=Yes

State	Party's Consent Required	Coverage of Participants Limited	Coverage of Jurors
Alabama	Y	Y	B
Alaska	C	N	N
Arizona	N	N	B
Arkansas	Y	Y	N
California	N	N	N
Colorado	N	N	B
Connecticut	N	Y	B
Delaware	N	N	–
District of Columbia	–	–	–
Florida	N	N	Y
Georgia	N	Y	B
Hawaii	N	Y	N
Idaho	N	N	N
Illinois	N	N	–
Indiana	N	N	–
Iowa	C	Y	B
Kansas	N	Y	B
Kentucky	N	N	Y
Louisiana	N	N	–
Maine	N	Y	N
Maryland	N-A/Y-T	Y	Y
Massachusetts	N	N	B
Michigan	N	Y	N
Minnesota	N-A/Y-T	Y	N
Mississippi	N	N	-
Missouri	N	Y	N

State	Party's Consent Required	Coverage of Participants Limited	Coverage of Jurors
Montana	N	N	Y
Nebraska	N	N	–
Nevada	N	N	B
New Hampshire	N	N	U
New Jersey	N	Y	B
New Mexico	N	Y	N
New York	N	N	–
North Carolina	N	Y	N
North Dakota	N	Y	N
Ohio	N	Y	Y
Oklahoma	C	Y	U
Oregon	N	Y	N
Pennsylvania	N	Y	–
Rhode Island	N	N	B
South Carolina	N	N	B
South Dakota	N	N	-
Tennessee	N	Y	N
Texas	Y	N	–
Utah	N	N	N
Vermont	N	N	B
Virginia	N	Y	N
Washington	N	N	Y
West Virginia	N	N	Y
Wisconsin	N	Y	B
Wyoming	N	Y	N

(Reprinted by permission of the Radio-Television News Directors Association, 2002. RTNDA has compiled a comprehensive guide of current law governing cameras in the courtroom. The guide details what courts in each state allow from the most permissive to the most restrictive. The state-by-state guide is available at http://www.rtnda.org/foi/scc.shtml)

Next, the federal guidelines restrict camera coverage of jurors. Similarly, few states currently allow unrestricted coverage of jurors.

The third section of the guidelines deals with equipment and personnel. As in most states allowing coverage, only one television camera operated by one camera person is permitted in trials compared with two of each in an appellate court. Similarly, only one still photographer with one camera is allowed. If more than one media outlet wishes coverage, the guidelines require pooling arrangements be made in advance and all disputes be mediated by the head of the pool.

This section of the federal guidelines also prohibits logos or insignia. Also, camera operators must wear proper business attire.

Although this restriction is found in only a handful of state guidelines, common sense would suggest all professionals present themselves well—and inconspicuously—at all times. For males, a coat and tie is considered proper; for females, a suit or conservative dress. Under no conditions should any professional enter a courtroom wearing clothing with slogans, pictures, or anything that would distract from the dignity of the proceedings.

Section four of the guidelines requires that equipment not produce any distracting sound or light, and Section five that equipment and personnel remain stationary in designated locations in the courtroom at all times. Entering and leaving the courtroom is reserved for before or after court proceedings or during recesses. Most states include these provisions in their guidelines as well. (See Figure 9.1: Courtroom Camera Guidelines.)

The last sections of the federal guidelines are reminders that media representatives who fail to comply are subject to sanctions (such as contempt citations). Also, the guidelines limit review regarding granting or denial of permission for camera coverage. These provisions are also commonly found in state guidelines.

Other issues may be covered in more detail in the guidelines of the various states. For example, one controversial topic is whether the news media might be required to make videotapes of coverage available to the court or to lawyers or either side as evidence supporting an appeal of a verdict.

Be sure you are familiar with the guidelines for the jurisdiction in which you are working. Have a copy of them with you at all times you are covering a trial.

With all fifty states allowing courtroom coverage, and cameras now in some federal courts, it is obvious courtroom cameras are here to stay. A new

Figure 9.2

Cameras in the Courtroom

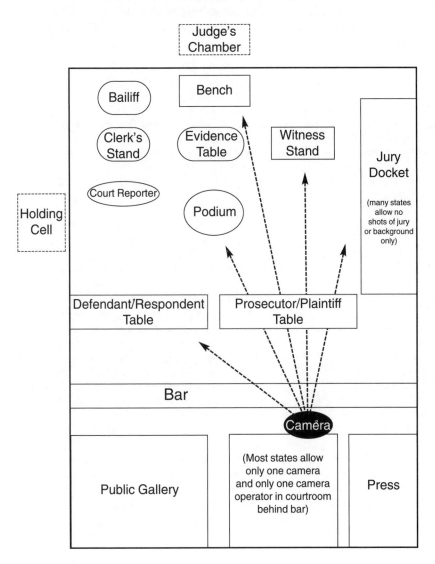

era has begun, and journalists must apply themselves to employing effectively this hard-won privilege, while keeping in sight the goal of enhancing public understanding without interfering with the process of judicial administration (the goal of any journalist, regardless of the presence or absence of cameras). Specific suggestions on how this goal may be attained are the subject of the final chapter, chapter 10.

NOTES

1. National Center for State Courts, "Summary of Television in the State Courts," figure 2.1. See also Radio-Television News Directors Association. "News Media Coverage of Judicial Proceedings with Cameras and Microphones," figure 9.2.

2. Federal Rules of Criminal Procedure, Rule 53.

3. Sunshine in the Courtroom Act, 105th Cong, 1st sess, HR 1280, 1997; Judicial Reform Act, 2000, HR 1252; and S 986, HR 2519, 107th Cong, A Bill to Allow Media Coverage of Court Proceedings, 2001.

4. Molly Treadway Johnson, "Electronic Media Coverage of Federal Civil Proceedings," manuscript, 1993; and Molly Treadway Johnson, "Electronic Media Coverage of Courtroom Proceedings," manuscript, 1994. See also "Summary of the Report of the Judicial Conference Committee on Cameras in Courtroom," manuscript, September 1990.

5. See Susanna Barber, *News Cameras in the Courtroom* (Norwood, N.J.: Ablex, 1987) for studies through 1987. See S. L. Alexander, "Cameras in the Courtroom," *Judicature* 74:6 (April–May 1991): 307–313; and S. L. Alexander, *"Mischievous Potentialities,"* PhD diss., University of Florida, 1990, for more recent cases. See also Graham, "Doing Justice," 32–37; Tony Mauro, "The Camera-Shy Federal Courts," *Media Studies Journal* 12:1 (Winter 1998): 60–65; David Harris, "The Appearance of Justice," *Arizona Law Review* 35 (1993): 785–827; "Television Coverage of State Criminal Trials," *St. Thomas Law Review* 9 (1997): 505–516; Ronald Goldfarb, *TV or Not TV* (New York: New York University Press, 1998); and Marjorie Cohn and David Dow, *Cameras in the Courtroom* (Jefferson, N.C.: McFarland and Company, 1998).

6. "Court TV Gains Approval," *Broadcasting and Cable*, 17 July 2000, 20–24; and "About Court TV," www.courttv.com (accessed 2002).

7. Court TV, "Facts and Opinions About Cameras in Courtrooms," manuscript, July 1995. See also S. L. Alexander, "The Impact of *California v Simpson* on Cameras in the Courtroom," *Judicature* 79:4 (January–February 1996): 169–172 (fifty-state survey found despite speculation, case had little effect on progress of camera usage).

8. *New York v Boss*, 261 A D 211 (NY Sup Ct Albany Cty), 2000.

9. Robert Waters, "Technology Can Remove Barriers to Free Information," *Brechner Report* (February 1998): 4.

10. *Florida v Egan*, cited in Gail Ramsey and Kristen McGuire, "Litigation Publicity," *Communications and the Law* (September 2000): 75. See also Deborah Sharp, "Web-Wired Courtroom Lets World Attend Fla Trial," *USA Today*, 17 August 1999, 3A.

11. Fredric Lederer, *The Road to the Virtual Courtroom?* (Williamsburg, Va.: State Justice Institute/William and Mary Law School, 1999).

Chapter Ten

Covering the Courts

Dunagin's People

"The jury recommends the death sentence
for the first person who writes a book
about this case."

Fair trial/free press considerations are a concern for members of the judiciary and the bar as well as for members of the press. In chapter 6, lawyers' and judges' canons of ethics and professional standards, particularly restrictions in their contact with the press, were discussed in some detail. Professional press organizations including the Society of Professional Journalists (SPJ), the Radio-TV News Directors Association (RTNDA), and the National Press

Photographers Association (NPPA) have developed detailed codes of ethics for their members (see appendix A).

Additionally, dozens of sources—including the American Bar Association, the National Center for State Courts, the National Judicial College Center for the Courts and Media, and such press groups as the Reporters Committee for Freedom of the Press—have gathered suggestions to help make cooperation easier for the benefit of all concerned with press coverage of the judicial process.[1] A discussion of these general suggestions along with those offered by judges, lawyers, court officials, and journalistic veterans of courtroom coverage follows.

WORKING WITH LAWYERS

At least two dozen writers—mostly lawyers—have published articles with such titles as "How to Manipulate the Media."[2] Many lawyers, trained to deal with all steps in the judicial process as adversarial transactions, carry over this approach in their exchanges with members of the press. There is even a growing field of "Litigation Public Relations" to help a lawyer deal with the court of public opinion.[3]

A few constant themes may be noted in these articles. On the positive side, lawyers are repeatedly warned never to lie to the press. As commentator Robert Wieder noted in a widely quoted 1994 article, there are three good reasons not to lie to the media:

> They will find out.
> They will be furious.
> Remember Nixon?[4]

However, most of the tips for handling the press suggest many lawyers have little respect for journalists and assume journalists are biased against their clients, arrogant, insensitive, and, most significantly, ignorant of the realities of the judicial process. ("Reporters are not rocket scientists when it comes to the law" is one of the more subtle comments occasionally overheard.)

Moreover, many lawyers assume they are much smarter than journalists and can have their way with them. One of the most frequent suggestions to lawyers being interviewed is simply to ignore a journalist's questions and instead repeat the answer to a different question, one that will better serve the client's interest.

Pulitzer Prize–winning US Supreme Court correspondent for the *New York*

Times, Linda Greenhouse, suggests the journalist might say, "Maybe you misunderstood me. What I really need to know is. . . ."[5]

Associated Press Special Correspondent Linda Deutsch, whose coverage of the Simpson criminal case was nominated for a Pulitzer Prize, says, "Lawyers tend to lump all reporters together. They don't differentiate between the pros and those who just hit and run and may ask stupid questions."[6]

Nina Totenberg is an award-winning legal affairs correspondent for National Public Radio (NPR). She says the tactic works "if the reporter isn't very good. . . . You just can't let them get away with it, you don't use it." Totenberg suggests, "When they complain, you say they didn't respond to what you wanted to know."[7]

Lawyers are also encouraged to repeat a few key phrases to control the "spin" on a story. For instance, celebrity criminal defense lawyer Robert Shapiro suggests: "The less choice you give the news director or reporter, the greater chance you have of airing the precise words you want aired. . . . Repeat them continuously and they will be repeated by the media. After a while, the repetition almost becomes a fact. That is your ultimate goal."[8]

CNN's Tim O'Brien (longtime ABC-TV legal correspondent), a lawyer as well as a journalist, says of Shapiro's advice: "Sometimes they do that. I'll listen to what they have to say, sometimes it's just as usable."[9]

Fred Graham, a lawyer who worked as a journalist for the *New York Times* and CBS-TV before becoming managing editor and chief anchor of Court TV, says "All news sources try to manipulate you. . . . Figure out where the hostilities are."[10]

Pamela Coyle, a graduate of the Yale Law School MLS program for journalists covering legal topics, says, "I find the biggest asset in not being manipulated is to know the case and know the record."[11]

According to Tony Mauro, longtime Supreme Court correspondent who currently works for American Lawyer Media, "Spin control has invaded this beat just like any other." Mauro says, "I know when I'm being spun, and I take it with a grain of salt. I write it the way I see it and just quote them and let them have their say."[12]

Wendell Gauthier, a celebrated class action plaintiff's lawyer, won billion-dollar awards against such companies as Shell Oil. According to him, "Lawyers don't manipulate journalists. Most journalists are lazy. If I give 'em the whole story, they love it."[13]

To avoid even the appearance of being manipulated—or being rightly called lazy—here are some further suggestions for journalists:

Do not feel obligated to limit your reporting to the lawyer's selected "sound bites." Politely request that the lawyer answer the question you asked: make it clear you will not settle for less.

Do not let the lawyer confuse you with legal jargon. Ask him to explain in layman's terms. (See the Glossary.)
If the case is taken on appeal, ask the lawyer for a copy of the briefs submitted rather than merely relying on his verbal description of their contents.
Do not rely on the lawyer's good will. Follow up on all proceedings.

Lawyers are also advised to "schmooze" or cultivate (or even feign) friendliness with journalists assigned to court coverage. That way, they hope to avoid what commentators have described as being crucified in the press.

Do not be taken in by a well-prepared lawyer. He may flatter you by knowing your name and the highlights of your career, but never forget he is sworn to represent only one point of view, while your role is to present balanced coverage.
As discussed in chapter 6, a journalist should be wary of manipulation by lawyers, particularly in a high-profile criminal case. Carefully "leaked" information (such as the existence of improperly obtained confessions, which would not be admissible in a trial) can prejudice a defendant's right to a fair trial with an impartial jury.

Freelance author and journalist Joseph Bosco, who wrote a book on the Simpson trial, says a reporter develops a sixth sense to detect a lawyer's attempts to manipulate him. According to Bosco, it's a mutual seduction, since the reporter is also trying to obtain information from the lawyer. Bosco says the machinations during the Simpson trial were "an incredible dance, with a pecking order as well-defined as a cocktail party. The only thing not being passed around were the hors d'oeuvres and drinks."[14]

Pulitzer Prize–winning *New York Times* writer Rick Bragg doesn't like giving advice, but he's willing to say what works for him. Regarding lawyers' attempts to manipulate reporters with "leaks," Bragg says his allegiance is to the reader: "Once in a while they leak information. . . . I don't care if it floated in on the wings of a dove, if it's solid and helps the reader, I'll use it."[15]

Linda Deutsch reminds reporters: "Any journalist should know all lawyers are salesmen, salesmen there to sell their cases, either side—they are attempting to sell and they'll try to sell to you." Deutsch adds: "Most are glib talkers. That's fine for the jurors, but reporters should be wary."[16]

According to Maurice Possley, author and award-winning court reporter for the *Chicago Tribune*, "No matter what the lawyers say in the hallway, it's what they say in the courthouse that counts. They can put any spin on it . . . that doesn't change what happened in the courthouse."[17]

Lawyers are also advised to avoid actually saying the words, "No comment." They know they will be treated better if they find an excuse for the failure to answer a question, such as, "We don't want to try this case outside the courtroom before the trial starts."

Pamela Coyle suggests a journalist might use the records as leverage to get the parties to talk: "Gee, it looks from the record like you are saying your opponent encouraged a witness to lie. What led you to that conclusion?"[18]

Don Ray, accomplished at ferreting out information and author of *Checking Out Lawyers*,[19] suggests a journalist employ the "ratchet" approach in dealing with a reluctant source. Ray says a journalist might bypass the lawyer and approach the client directly, saying, "I note you filed this case. May I quote you as saying you did file it?" After the source agrees, Ray says the journalist keeps tightening the ratchet: "May I quote you as saying you hope to win your case?" According to Ray, before he knows it, the source is chatting away about the details of the case.[20]

If a lawyer seems reluctant to be interviewed, reasons you might cite why it would be beneficial to speak with you include the need to protect a client in the arena of public opinion, to enhance the public's understanding of the judicial system, and, incidentally, to boost the prominence of the lawyer in the public eye.

If a lawyer still refuses to help, you might point out (assuming it is true) the opposing lawyer is cooperative, and he is doing a disservice to his client by failing to help you balance your presentation.

Do not feel forced to accept an evasive answer as if it were responsive to your question. Make it clear that you recognize the lawyer is evading a direct answer even if he does not use the exact words "No Comment."

One area in which lawyers seem to receive conflicting advice is that of speaking "off the record." Some legal commentators suggest (wisely) to assume everything is "on the record" when someone is speaking to a reporter.

You are not obligated to agree to accepting any strictures on what you may publish or broadcast. But if you choose to do so, make it very clear exactly what is "on" or "off" the record—spell out exactly what you mean by those phrases and do not violate your agreement in this regard.

Joe Bosco says if he told everything he knew about a high-profile case such as the Simpson trial, he could sell a million books, but he gave his word some of the information was off the record—and he regards his word as a matter of honor.[21]

Senior editor for online *Slate*, Dahlia Lithwick, says it's a "huge issue" for her, because people know she is a lawyer and want to confide in her, but she never wants word to get out she can't be trusted: "It's like a deposit in a trust bank. If I keep a confidence once, twice, three times, somewhere down the line there'll be a payoff."[22]

Lyle Denniston, author of a book on court coverage and an experienced reporter on the US Supreme Court, told lawyers at a National Press Club gathering "How to Deal With Journalists." He says that just because he will honor a commitment not to print some information with the lawyer as a source at the lawyer's request, it does not mean he might not try to obtain the information elsewhere.[23]

Some commentators have suggested a lawyer should "pull rank" on a journalist by suggesting he will go above the journalist's head to an editor or news director in regard to conflicts over coverage.

Do not let a lawyer threaten you by pointing out his client is a heavy advertiser or by threatening to sue you. Tell him to deal with the advertising or legal departments of your organization (which will surely let you know whether you are going too far for your employer's comfort).

Another technique lawyers are advised to follow to delay unfavorable stories on their clients is to provide the journalist with voluminous documents at the last minute and to stall on promised interviews with clients (particularly that elusive promised "exclusive"). Ted Gest, head of the Criminal Justice Journalists organization and experienced legal affairs writer for *US News and World Report* among other publications, says the document tactic might work for a few hours, but not in the long run: "Most journalists are experienced with absorbing large amounts of documents in a short time period. I and many others have managed on a deadline basis."[24]

Regarding the interview tactic, Tim O'Brien says, "It's most irritating. They could call and say 'I'm not going to talk to you for a certain reason.' Jerking a reporter around only arouses ill will."[25]

Lawyers have been advised to insist on seeing a copy of the journalist's work before it is published or broadcast.

Offer to double-check the accuracy of any direct quotes, particularly those involving highly controversial issues if the lawyer will agree to an interview, but do not ever show a subject advance copies of edited work.
If you want to interview a litigant, it is usually a good idea to contact him

through his lawyer. This is especially true in criminal cases in which your access to an incarcerated defendant is limited.
*Remember that the real story is in the court record and the court proceedings. There is no such thing as being overprepared for coverage.

A journalist should remember that he will be repeatedly returning to the office of the prosecutor for future stories, so it would pay to build up good relationships with employees of the office. Similarly, the office of the public defender along with a handful of private criminal defense lawyers generally handle the majority of cases processed through the criminal justice system in a journalist's geographical area.

Ziva Branstetter, who covered courts for the *Tulsa World*, reminds journalists to cultivate bailiffs and clerks as well as lawyers: "Give them some inside information so they will help you."[26]

Columbia Journalism School graduate James Varney, a veteran courtroom reporter, agrees, adding that deputies assigned to guard defendants in a criminal case can supply a journalist with colorful details that add to the story.[27]

Richard Angelico, who won the Society of Professional Journalists Award for his coverage of courts for WDSU (NBC)-TV, suggests a journalist "make friends with everyone." Angelico adds: "Most who work in the courts are people dying to tell you what they know. Give them a chance to blurt it all out."[28]

WORKING WITH JUDGES

In addition to the discussion in chapter 6 regarding obligations of judges in meeting professional canons and standards of conduct, some additional tips are useful in working with judges.

As mentioned earlier, the National Center for State Courts prepared a *Manual for Managing Notorious Trials* for judges. Journalists might ask to work with the trial judge, who, it is suggested, should follow techniques such as the following:

*Meeting ahead of time with news media representatives; treating all members of the media equally and fairly; not appearing excessively friendly with individual members of the media.
*Establishing in writing clear ground rules; accommodating the media with information such as the court's schedule, timing of decisions, and other procedural matters on a daily basis.

*Selecting a single source to speak for the judge, either a member of the court staff or a representative of the media serving as a liaison.
*Doing nothing to become the focus of personal attention.
*Being available on a daily basis to clarify issues of the legal process (naturally offering no opinions on evidence or the merits of the case).[29]

The National Judicial College Center for the Courts and Media in Reno also gathered tips for judges dealing with members of the news media and distributed them at a conference on "Media and the Courts." Judges were advised to treat reporters courteously, to be wary of reacting with quick "off-the-top" responses, and to expect critical comments to be answered in subsequent news coverage by persons or agencies criticized.[30]

An accompanying "News Media Checklist for Communication with Judges" included tips for reporters such as giving the judge time to review the material before an interview; remembering the prohibition against commenting on pending litigation in the Code of Judicial Conduct; and having a plan of action, complete with legal advice, if communication with the court breaks down and the journalist feels his rights have been violated.[31]

The conference concluded with issuance of "Top 10 Significant Issues on Court-Media Issues." Among them are the need for judges to encourage interdisciplinary educational opportunities; to seek other remedies than gag orders; to assume cameras should be allowed in courtrooms except in extraordinary cases; to explain, on the record, the reasons for their rulings; and to encourage media organizations to develop an ombudsman system to hear recommendations from the courts and public whenever feasible.[32]

A journalist would do well to adopt a cooperative attitude toward the court, particularly prior to coverage of high-profile trials. For example, judges might benefit from some sort of pre-trial checklist. A journalist might suggest a TV news director or editor—along with camera operators, photographers, and reporters involved—meet with the judge well in advance to prepare such a checklist.

Some states have drawn up voluntary Bench-Bar-Press guidelines. The journalist should be aware of any such guidelines in his state, and that in at least one noted case, journalists were found in contempt of court for failing to follow supposedly voluntary guidelines.[33]

Some issues the press might want to resolve ahead of time with the court:

*Handling of access to the courtroom (seating passes) and to printed documents by the clerk's office in a fair, orderly fashion. Information packets might include some sort of fact sheet (with names, addresses, and phone

*numbers of the judge, lawyers, and court administrators involved in the
case), the indictment or information, lists of potential witnesses, press coverage policies, and of course courtroom camera guidelines.*

**Designation of areas where cameras may remain set up for interviews at*
*recesses and before or after court proceedings. Most state guidelines do not
allow cameras in courtrooms unless the judge is presiding at the time.*

**Availability of photocopying equipment and telephones for press use—*
*demonstrating compliance with the guidelines for camera coverage in most
states, which require any extra expense incurred must be paid for by the
members of the press pool (who should be required to sign an agreement to
do so in advance of ordering equipment).*

**Setting up some sort of center with video and audio feeds—or, at minimum,*
*audio feeds—of courtroom activities for those unable to obtain access to the
courtroom itself.*

**Distribution of special parking permits for the press requiring large vans,*
*microwave transmitters, or other remote equipment and possibly for repre-
sentatives transporting heavy equipment in news cars or private vehicles.*

New York's Chief Judge Judith Kaye, who announced the "Standards of
Civility" for lawyers in her state (discussed in chapter 6), issued what she
called a "plea for more complete, more informed, more balanced coverage of
courts. . . . More informed coverage, in many cases, may require some background in the courts and their procedures."[34]

US Appeal Court Judge Pierre Leval (Second Circuit) says that the competition to get into print and capture audiences may elevate sensationalism
above accuracy. And Judge Leval wonders why reporters handling compli-
cated court stories often seem unwilling to check with their sources, particularly for accurate quotes.[35]

Linda Greenhouse agrees: "Don't be afraid to ask questions when you
don't understand, ask right away. Don't try to look smart."[36]

Judge Hiller Zobel, who as associate justice of Massachusetts Superior
Court presided over the high-profile "Nanny Trial" of British babysitter Lou-
ise Woodward in Boston, added to the controversy when he reduced her conviction from second-degree murder to manslaughter.[37] Judge Zobel said,
"There's no reason why a judge can't talk about the fundamentals of a case
. . . as long as the judge isn't commenting on the case itself." He adds, "I did
that in the Woodward trial, where a lot of English journalists didn't really
understand the procedures. Several of them were kind enough to say it helped
them."[38]

Harvard Law Professor Alan Dershowitz pulls no punches: "I think the coverage of courts in America is an absolute disaster, with no exceptions. The reason it's a disaster is that there's not a journalist in America who's prepared to look at motives of judges, to look behind the opinions." Dershowitz, who wrote a book on the background of the US Supreme Court justices' handling of the 2000 election case, *Bush v Gore*, suggests, "Judges are politicians and ought to be treated like other politicians."[39]

Two federal appeal court judges, Judge Gilbert Merritt (Sixth Circuit) and Judge Richard Arnold (Eighth Circuit), were interviewed on the topic of reciprocity between the press and judiciary. Judge Merritt said, "I think that the press needs to have better standards and take into account the interest of the system of justice in our society, in addition to just the momentary interest in getting it out to the public to beat some competition."[40]

Judge Arnold, who once worked as a newspaper reporter, said, "[J]udges would do well to try to cultivate a constructive relationship with the press."[41]

According to Judge Zobel, some problems are the result of the current trend of covering trials as entertainment, with TV coverage particularly demanding commentary. He describes watching a talk program during the Woodward trial with three different pundits describing what "Zobel has to be thinking" and talking to back to the TV: "Hey, I'm Judge Zobel, and I'm not thinking any of that!"[42]

ENTERPRISE STORIES

In addition to day-to-day trial coverage, the journalist might wish to develop original "enterprise" stories on broad, court-related themes. Some possibilities for stories on lawyers might include the following:

For elected district attorneys or public defenders: note win-loss record, particularly for lawyers who seem to drop cases more frequently than necessary or who never seem to take a case to trial. Also: are all the assistant DAs from the DA's law school? Is there diversity in race/gender of ADAs?

For public defenders: caseloads may be unreasonably high and pay unreasonably low. Or there may be evidence of abuse of indigents by those representing them pro bono. Check whether those repeatedly appointed to lucrative cases are generous donors to judges' campaign coffers.

For private lawyers: are there patterns such as an inordinate number of requests for continuances, possibly an abuse of clients' rights? In heavily advertised contingency cases, such as accident cases in which the lawyer could receive as much as half of the damages awarded, does the "name" lawyer actually handle cases himself from initial consultation through trial?

Similarly, enterprise stories on judges might include the following:

Quality ratings of judges by the local bar association. If the local bar does not publish such information, the journalist might conduct such a survey.
A comparative study of the type of penalties given out by various judges. For instance, some judges seem frequently to suspend sentences; "hanging judges" often impose maximum sentences; some accept plea bargains more readily than others; and some seem to favor plaintiffs whereas others seem to favor defendants. Is there a pattern of animosity between certain judges and certain lawyers?
Judges' campaigns for office: are their major donors lawyers who frequently appear before them? Conversely, particularly if judges are appointed: the record of political contributions by judges to politicians.
A description of how judges are assigned to various cases and possible political influences on the process.

Finally, the journalist should not forget general enterprise stories and features on the court. A useful source of inspiration for enterprise stories may be found in government agencies' websites, some of which have been mentioned previously. These include the Administrative Office of the US Courts (www.uscourts.gov), where Public Affairs Specialist Dick Carelli, longtime legal affairs reporter, is especially helpful and can be reached at 202–502–2601; the Bureau of Justice Statistics (http://ojp.usdoj.gov); the Federal Judicial Center (www.fjc.gov); the US Department of Justice (http://ojp.usdoj.gov); the US Sentencing Commission (www.ussc.gov); the US Supreme Court (www.supremecourt.gov); and other government websites mentioned earlier such as PACER, Public Access to Court Electronic Records (http://pacer.psc.uscourt.gov),

Other useful websites include the National Center for State Courts (www.ncsconline.org) and the National Judicial College Center for the Courts and Media (www.judges.org). For information on lawyers, see the American Bar Association (www.abanet.org), the American Board of Trial Advocates (www.abota.org), the National Association of Attorneys General (www.naag.org), the National Association of Criminal Defense Lawyers (www.nacdl.org), the National District Attorneys Association (www.ndaa.org), and both the Martindale Hubbell lawyers' directory (www.martindale.com) and the West Legal Directory (http://directory.findlaw.com).

Fee/free databases including FindLaw (www.findlaw.com), West Doc (www.westdoc.com), Lexis One (www.lexisone.com), and American Media Lawyer's Law.com (www.law.com), as well as Court TV (www.courttv.com), are filled with story ideas as are those of various press organizations, including the Criminal Justice Journalists (www.reporters.net/cjj), Reporter's Committee for Freedom of the Press (www.rcfp.org), the Investigative Reporters and Editors (www.ire.org), the Society of Professional Journalists (www.spj.org), and the Radio TV News Directors Association (www.rtn-da.org).

Tony Mauro, longtime reporter on the US Supreme Court beat, suggests journalists looking for story ideas might localize Supreme Court stories. He says the local office of the district attorney or city attorney, the state attorney general, or the local chapter of the American Civil Liberties Union may have a special interest in cases in the Supreme Court.[43]

Harvard Law's Alan Dershowitz suggests journalists take the time to do more in-depth stories, particularly on appeal court decisions, especially those of the US Supreme Court. "Look at realities. Look at law clerks who write the decisions, who they are, how they are picked," he suggests.[44]

Pulitzer Prize–winning writer Thomas French of the *St. Petersburg Times* emphasizes the power of narrative in the longer piece or series, telling a story in chronological order. He reminds journalists to ask themselves: what should readers take with them from your story?[45]

Stories on budgets and other administrative issues related to running the courts are very informative. Individuals in the courthouse ranging from security personnel through judges may have colorful stories to tell. Explaining court procedures in general, particularly prior to a high-profile trial, will help the public better understand the process of judicial administration.

CONCLUSION

As emphasized earlier, the journalist must work hard to do a good job covering courts. Howard Mintz, *San Jose Mercury-News* legal affairs reporter, reminds journalists that they must understand the courts before they can explain the courts to others: "The most important thing is to learn how the court works, the basic steps in a case . . . all your coverage is then a lot easier."[46]

Remember the importance of accuracy. Double-check all your work. Spell everyone's name correctly. Be mindful of the legal community's pet peeves. Translate all legalese. Identify all sources for stories. Keep up with dockets and follow up on stories. Study the judicial system.

Award-winning Associated Press legal reporter Tim Talley, formerly of the *Baton Rouge (La.) Advocate*, said a good journalist should "do his legal research. Read the criminal code, the statutes. Know the legal issues."[47]

Eve Burton, former assistant general counsel for the New York *Daily News* and currently at Columbia University, reminded reporters to remember how important it is that they think to the future. Burton said reporters should carry court access cards with them at all times: "Push for access no matter how small the case. Rights are won and lost on small cases."[48]

Jane Okrasinski, a lawyer who worked as a producer/reporter for Court TV, also insisted a reporter should keep in mind the big picture: "Journalists should be deferential in regard to the needs of lawyers and judges and respectful of the judicial process."[49]

Courtroom reporter for the *Seattle Times*, Duff Wilson, emphasized that a journalist should "make the extra effort to be fair to everyone, including hostile subjects, and then call them again after the story is published."[50]

NPR's Nina Totenberg emphasizes the need for thorough research in covering courts: "Really be prepared before you go into the trial, or onto the beat. Don't take the word of anyone, even a seasoned reporter or the law clerk. Check it out."[51]

In the foreword to Theo Wilson's book of anecdotes on Wilson's decades of covering courts for the New York *Daily News*, *Headline Justice,* Linda Deutsch came up with what she calls the Theo Wilson Cardinal Rules of Trial Coverage, which include the following:

*Never leave the courtroom except to file your story; you might miss a crucial moment.
*Don't give undue attention to out-of-court gossip; the only important facts are those that come from the witness stand to the jury's ears.
*And, most importantly, never come to a trial with your mind made up; listen to the evidence as if you were a juror and report it with a fair, unbiased approach.[52]

Lawyer Lincoln Caplan described what he called "The Failure (and Promise) of Legal Journalism": Courtroom journalism generally stresses personalities of court participants over ideas, narrowly focuses on proceedings, and often is presented in sports style, complete with play-by-play. Caplan concluded that journalists today need to provide a frame of reference for their coverage, particularly for live broadcast coverage of courts.[53]

The Freedom Forum's First Amendment Center completed a study on the press and the justice system that found other problems with coverage included overuse of unidentified sources and reliance on leaks; no explanation of why juries, lawyers, or judges do what they do; and tendency to describe constitutional rights as "technicalities." The study concluded: "The Constitution's promise of a fair trial cannot be left entirely to the courts to fulfill, since courts at every level have shown themselves vulnerable to prejudice, pressure, and (occasionally) corruption. As part of its First Amendment duty, the press is responsible for keeping a watchful eye regularly trained on court performance—a duty it is not currently fulfilling."[54]

In sum, the journalist must maintain respect for the court system and never forget his main purpose is to inform the public about a process designed to administer justice. A trial is not held to entertain the public, and press coverage should not interfere with the Constitutional right to a fair trial. However, freedom of the press is also a Constitutional right and a duty, and a professional journalist needs to keep these mandates in mind when covering courtrooms and the process of judicial administration.

NOTES

1. See, for example, American Bar Association, *Facts about the American Judicial System* (Chicago: ABA, 1999); American Bar Association, *Fair Trial/Free Press Voluntary Agreements* (Chicago: ABA, 1974); American Bar Association, *A Journalist's Guide to Civil Procedure* (videocassette) (Chicago: ABA, 1993); American Bar Association, *A Journalist's Guide to Federal Criminal Procedure* (videocassette) (Chicago: ABA, 1989); American Bar Association, *A Journalist's Primer on Civil Procedure* (Chicago: ABA, 1993); American Bar Association, *A Journalist's Primer on Federal Criminal Procedure* (Chicago: ABA, 1988); American Bar Association, *Law and the Courts* (Chicago: ABA, 1987); American Bar Association, *Model Rules of Professional Conduct and Code of Judicial Conduct* (Chicago: ABA, 1989); American Bar Association, *The Rights of Fair Trial and Free Press* (Chicago: ABA, 1981); American Bar Association, *Standards for Criminal Justice*, 3rd ed. (Chicago: ABA, 1992); The ABA and the National Conference of Lawyers and Representatives of the Media, *The Reporter's Key* (Chicago: ABA, 1994); Norm Goldstein, ed., *The Associated Press Stylebook and Briefing on Media Law* (Cambridge, Mass.: Perseus, 2000); ASNE/ANPA, *Free Press and Fair Trial* (Washington, D.C.: ASNE/SNPA, 1982); Rebecca Fanning, "The Court Officer: Meet the Press," *Media Studies Journal* 6:1 (Winter 1992): 94–103; The Florida Bar Association, *Reporter's Handbook* (Tallahassee: FBA, 1991); Jerianne Hayslett, *Tips for a Successful Media Plan on High Profile Trials* (Los Angeles: LAVO Courts of LA City, 1993); *NJ Reporter's Handbook on Press Law and the Courts* (Trenton: NJ Press Association/Bar Foundation, 1990); Albert Pickerell, ed., *The Courts and the News Media* (San Francisco: California Judges Association, 1984); Donald Pollock, "Issues in Sensational or Widely Publicized Cases," manuscript, Administrative Office of the Courts Legal Division (Miami, Fla.), 1990; RCFP, *The First Amendment Handbook*, Washington, D.C. (periodic); Fredric Tulsky, "Courts," in *The Reporter's Handbook*, ed. John Ullmann and Jan Colbert (IRE), 2nd ed. (New York: St. Martin's Press, 1991), 315–346; and Steve Weinberg (IRE), "Investigating Government: The Judicial System," in *The Reporter's Handbook,* ed. John Ullmann and Jan Colbert (IRE), 3rd ed. (New York: St. Martin's Press, 1996), 217–269.

2. See Robert Bennett, "Press Advocacy and the High-Profile Client," *Loyola of LA Law Review* 30:7 (November 1996): 13–20; Robert Boland and Kennard Strutin, "Media

Relations for the Criminal Defense Lawyer," *The Practical Litigator* (July 1993): 59–70; Nancy Boles and Katherine Heaviside, "When a Reporter Calls," *ABA Journal* 73 (1 June 1987): 90–94; Ken Bresler, "How to Handle Reporters," *The Florida Bar Journal* (November 1988): 23–24; Andrew Cohen, "Lessons from the Timothy McVeigh Trial II," *Media Studies Journal* 12:1 (Winter 1998): 14–17; William Colby, "When the Media Calls," *The Kansas Journal of Law and Public Policy* (Spring 1995): 77–80; Lee Cooper, "Don't Get Trampled By Media Circus," *ABA Journal* (February 1997): 8; Lyle Denniston, "How to Deal With Journalists," *The Washington Lawyer* (September/October 1995): 37ff.; *The Reporter and the Law*, 2nd ed. (New York: Columbia University Press, 1992, 1996); Clancy Dubos, "That Phone Call from Hell," *NOBA: Briefly Speaking* (Fall 1993): 22; Ken Fairchild, "Case by Case," *Texas Bar Journal* 58:5 (May 1995): 476–477; "The First Annual Symposium on Media and the Law," *South Dakota Law Review* 41 (1996): 79–130; Stuart Gold, "Litigators and the Press," *Litigation* (Winter 1987): 36ff; Thomas Hodson, "The Judge," in *Media Studies Journal* 6:1 (Winter 1992): 86–93; Roscoe Howard, "The Media, Attorneys, and Fair Criminal Trials," *The Kansas Journal of Law and Public Policy* (Spring 1995): 61–75; George Killenberg, "Into the Legal Maze," in *Public Affairs Reporting* (New York: St. Martin's Press, 1992), 205–262; Dick Krantz, "Covering the Courts," in *The Reporter's Handbook*, ed. John Ullmann and Steve Honeyman (IRE) (New York: St. Martin's Press, 1983), 359–393; Ronald Lovell, "Courts," 219–272, in *Reporting Public Affairs* (Prospect Heights, Ill.: Waveland Press, 1993); James Lukaszewski, "Managing Litigation Visibility: How to Avoid Lousy Trial Publicity," *Public Relations Quarterly* (Spring 1995): 28–24; Edward McCullum, "The Advocate and the Media," *Mercer Law Review* 42 (1991): 875–882; Tom Moran, "Rules and Commandments for Dealing with the Press," *Texas Bar Journal* 58:5 (May 1995): 471–473; Mark Moreland, "Defending the High Profile Client," *Trial* (April 1992): 24–31; Jonathan Moses, "Legal Spin Control," *Columbia Law Review* 95 (1995): 1811–1856; "Reporting on the Courts and the Law," manuscript, Florida Bar/American Judicature Society, September 1990, 13–15; "Reporting the Law," *Federal Rules and Decisions* 160 (18 June 1994): 406–423; Michael Riccardi, "Lawyers, Press Examine Each Profession's Values," *The Legal Intelligencer* 26 (September 1995): 1; Robert Shapiro, "Secrets of a Celebrity Lawyer," *Columbia Journalism Review* (September/October 1994): 25–29; "Shall We Dance?" *Judicature* 80:1 (July–August 1996): 30–42; Robert Stephen, "Prejudicial Publicity Surrounding a Criminal Trial," *Suffolk University Law Review* 26 (1992): 1063–1106; and Robert Wieder, "How to Manipulate the Media," *California Lawyer* (February 1994): 60–66.

3. Suzanne Roschwalb and Richard Stack, *Litigation Public Relations* (Littleton, Colo.: Rothman and Co., 1995). See also Dirk Gibson and Mariposa Podilla, "Litigation Public Relations Problems and Limits," *Public Relations Review* 28:2 (Summer 1999): 215–223; "Litigation Public Relations," *The Review of Litigation* 14 (1995): 595–618; John Watson, "Litigation Public Relations," *Communication Law and Policy* 7:51 (2000): 77–103.

4. Wieder, "How to Manipulate the Media," 25–29.

5. Linda Greenhouse, interview by the author, New Orleans, 24 October 2000.

6. Linda Deutsch, interview by the author, Los Angeles, August 1996; (telephone) 22 August 1996; and New Orleans, 6 October 1997. See Linda Deutsch and Michael Fleeman, *Verdict: The Chronicle of the OJ Simpson Trial* (Kansas City, Mo.: Associated Press, 1995).

7. Nina Totenberg, telephone interview by the author, 16 July 2002.

8. Robert Shapiro, "Secrets of a Celebrity Lawyer," 25–29.

9. Tim O'Brien, interview by the author, New Orleans, May 1997; and (telephone) 19 May 1997.

10. Fred Graham, interview by the author, New Orleans, 27 October 1997. See also Fred Graham, *Happy Talk* (New York: W. W. Norton, 1990).

11. Pamela Coyle, interview by the author, New Orleans, 5 March 1998.

12. Tony Mauro, interview by the author, Reno, 9 June 2000; and (telephone) 5 July 2002. See also Tony Mauro, "The Camera-Shy Federal Courts," *Media Studies Journal* 12:1 (Winter 1998): 60–65.

13. Wendell Gauthier, interview by the author, New Orleans, 15 October 1997. (Deceased December 2001).

14. Joseph Bosco, telephone interview by the author, 22 August 1996; and New Orleans, 24 November 1997. See Joseph Bosco, *A Problem of Evidence* (New York: William Morrow, 1996).

15. Rick Bragg, interview by the author, New Orleans, 3 July 2002.

16. Linda Deutsch, interview by the author.

17. Maurice Possley, interview by the author, Baton Rouge, Louisiana, 29 March 2000. See Maurice Possley and Rick Kogan, *Everybody Pays: Two Men, One Murder and the Price of Truth* (New York: Putnam's Sons, 2001).

18. Pamela Coyle, "Court Records," manuscript, IRE National Conference, 5 June 1998.

19. Don Ray, *Checking Out Lawyers* (Spartanburg, S.C.: Military Information Enterprises, 1997).

20. Don Ray, interview by the author, New Orleans, 5 June 1998.

21. Joseph Bosco, interview by the author.

22. Dahlia Lithwick, interview by the author, Reno, 9 June 2000; and (telephone) 22 June 2000.

23. Denniston, "How to Deal with Journalists," 37.

24. Ted Gest, interview by the author, Reno, 9 June 2000; and (telephone) 2 July 2002.

25. Tim O'Brien, interview by the author.

26. Ziva Branstetter, interview by the author, Lafayette, Louisiana, 30 March 1996.

27. James Varney, interview by the author, New Orleans, 17 September 1997.

28. Richard Angelico, interview by the author, New Orleans, 20 November and 3 December 1997.

29. Timothy Murphy, *A Manual for Managing Notorious Trials* (Williamsburg, Va.: National Center for State Courts, 1992, 1998), 37.

30. National Judicial College Center for the Courts and Media, "Media and the Courts," manuscript, NJC National Conference, 1996; and "Courts and Media—Conflict and Cooperation," manuscript, NJC National Conference, 2000.

31. National Judicial College, "Media and the Courts."

32. National Judicial College, "Media and the Courts."

33. *Federated v Swedburg*, 633 P 2d 74 (1981).

34. Honorable Judith Kaye, "The Third Branch and the Fourth Estate," *Media Studies Journal* 12:1 (Winter 1998): 77.

35. Honorable Pierre Leval, interview by the author, New Orleans, 14 April 1998.

36. Linda Greenhouse, interview by the author.

37. *Commonwealth v Woodward*, Supr Ct Mass Middlesex No 97–0433, 1997; *affm'd* 427 Mass 659, 1998.

38. Honorable Hiller Zobel, interview by the author, Reno, 9 June 2000; and (telephone) 22 July 2002. See Hiller Zobel, "Judicial Independence and the Need to Please," *The Judges Journal* (Fall 2001): 5–10.

39. Alan Dershowitz, interview by the author, New Orleans, 3 June 2002; and (telephone) 16 July 2002. See Alan Dershowitz, *Supreme Injustice: How the High Court Hijacked Election 2000* (New York: Oxford Press, 2001).

40. Honorable Gilbert Merritt, "Justice by the Consent of the Governed," *Media Studies Journal* 12:1 (Winter 1998): 86.

41. Honorable Richard Arnold, "Justice by the Consent of the Governed," 89–90.

42. Honorable Hiller Zobel, interview by the author.

43. Tony Mauro, cited in Evelyn Theriot, USWL: *SPJ Verite* (Autumn 1996): 12.

44. Alan Dershowtiz, interview by the author.

45. Tom French, interview by the author, Columbus, Ohio, 20 October 2000.

46. Howard Mintz, interview by the author, Baton Rouge, Louisiana, 29 March 2000.

47. Tim Talley, interview by the author, Lafayette, Louisiana, 30 March 1996.

48. Eve Burton, interview by the author, New Orleans, 5 June 1998.

49. Jane Okrasinksi, interview by the author, New Orleans, 22 May 1996.

50. Duff Wilson, interview by the author, 5 June 1998. See also "Covering Courts," manuscript, IRE National Conference, 5 June 1998.

51. Nina Totenberg, interview by the author.

52. Linda Deutsch, foreword in Theo Wilson, *Headline Justice* (New York: Thunder's Mouth Press, 1996), xiv.

53. Lincoln Caplan, "The Failure (and Promise) of Legal Journalism," in *Postmortem*, ed. Jeffrey Abramson (New York: Basic Books, 1996), 199–207.

54. Wallace Westfeldt and Tom Wicker, *Indictment: The News Media and the Criminal Justice System* (Nashville, Tenn.: First Amendment Center, 1998).

Appendix A: Codes of Ethics

SOCIETY OF PROFESSIONAL
JOURNALISTS CODE OF ETHICS

Preamble

Members of the Society of Professional Journalists believe that public enlightenment is the forerunner of justice and the foundation of democracy. The duty of the journalist is to further those ends by seeking truth and providing a fair and comprehensive account of events and issues. Conscientious journalists from all media and specialties strive to serve the public with thoroughness and honesty. Professional integrity is the cornerstone of a journalist's credibility.

Members of the Society share a dedication to ethical behavior and adopt this code to declare the Society's principles and standards of practice.

Seek Truth & Report It

Journalists should be honest, fair and courageous in gathering, reporting and interpreting information.

Journalists should:

- Test the accuracy of information from all sources and exercise care to avoid inadvertent error. Deliberate distortion is never permissible.
- Diligently seek out subjects of news stories to give them the opportunity to respond to allegations of wrongdoing.
- Identify sources whenever feasible. The public is entitled to as much information as possible on sources' reliability.

- Always question sources' motives before promising anonymity. Clarify conditions attached to any promise made in exchange for information. Keep promises.
- Make certain that headlines, news teases and promotional material, photos, video, audio, graphics, sound bites and quotations do not misrepresent. They should not oversimplify or highlight incidents out of context.
- Never distort the content of news photos or video. Image enhancement for technical clarity is always permissible. Label montages and photo illustrations.
- Avoid misleading re-enactments or staged news events. If re-enactment is necessary to tell a story, label it.
- Avoid undercover or other surreptitious methods of gathering information except when traditional open methods will not yield information vital to the public. Use of such methods should be explained as part of the story.
- Never plagiarize.
- Tell the story of the diversity and magnitude of the human experience boldly, even when it is unpopular to do so.
- Examine their own cultural values and avoid imposing those values on others.
- Avoid stereotyping by race, gender, age, religion, ethnicity, geography, sexual orientation, disability, physical appearance or social status.
- Support the open exchange of views, even views they find repugnant.
- Give voice to the voiceless; official and unofficial sources of information can be equally valid.
- Distinguish between advocacy and news reporting. Analysis and commentary should be labeled and not misrepresent fact or context.
- Distinguish news from advertising and shun hybrids that blur the lines between the two.
- Recognize a special obligation to ensure that the public's business is conducted in the open and that government records are open to inspection.

Minimize Harm

Ethical journalists treat sources, subjects and colleagues as human beings deserving of respect.

Journalists should:

- Show compassion for those who may be affected adversely by news coverage. Use special sensitivity when dealing with children and inexperienced sources or subjects.

- Be sensitive when seeking or using interviews or photographs of those affected by tragedy or grief.
- Recognize that gathering and reporting information may cause harm or discomfort. Pursuit of the news is not a license for arrogance.
- Recognize that private people have a greater right to control information about themselves than do public officials and others who seek power, influence or attention. Only an overriding public need can justify intrusion into anyone's privacy.
- Show good taste. Avoid pandering to lurid curiosity.
- Be cautious about identifying juvenile suspects or victims of sex crimes.
- Be judicious about naming criminal suspects before the formal filing of charges.
- Balance a criminal suspect's fair trial rights with the public's right to be informed.

Act Independently

Journalists should be free of obligation to any interest other than the public's right to know.

Journalists should:

- Avoid conflicts of interest, real or perceived.
- Remain free of associations and activities that may compromise integrity or damage credibility.
- Refuse gifts, favors, fees, free travel and special treatment, and shun secondary employment, political involvement, public office and service in community organizations if they compromise journalistic integrity.
- Disclose unavoidable conflicts.
- Be vigilant and courageous about holding those with power accountable.
- Deny favored treatment to advertisers and special interests and resist their pressure to influence news coverage.
- Be wary of sources offering information for favors or money; avoid bidding for news.

Be Accountable

Journalists are accountable to their readers, listeners, viewers and each other.

Journalists should:

- Clarify and explain news coverage and invite dialogue with the public over journalistic conduct.

- Encourage the public to voice grievances against the news media.
- Admit mistakes and correct them promptly.
- Expose unethical practices of journalists and the news media.
- Abide by the same high standards to which they hold others.

Courtesy Society of Professional Journalists, 2002. Reprinted with permission.

RADIO-TELEVISION NEWS DIRECTORS ASSOCIATION CODE OF ETHICS & PROFESSIONAL CONDUCT

The Radio-Television News Directors Association, wishing to foster the highest professional standards of electronic journalism, promote public understanding of and confidence in electronic journalism, and strengthen principles of journalistic freedom to gather and disseminate information, establishes this Code of Ethics and Professional Conduct.

PREAMBLE

Professional electronic journalists should operate as trustees of the public, seek the truth, report it fairly and with integrity and independence, and stand accountable for their actions.

PUBLIC TRUST

Professional electronic journalists should recognize that their first obligations are to the public.

Professional electronic journalists should:

- Understand that any commitment other than service to the public undermines trust and credibility.
- Recognize that service in the public interest creates an obligation to reflect the diversity of the community and guard against oversimplification of issues or events.
- Provide a full range of information to enable the public to make enlightened decisions.
- Fight to ensure that the public's business is conducted in public.

TRUTH

Professional electronic journalists should pursue truth aggressively and present the news accurately, in context, and as completely as possible.

Professional electronic journalists should:

- Continuously seek the truth.
- Resist distortions that obscure the importance of events.
- Clearly disclose the origin of information and label all material provided by outsiders.

Professional electronic journalists should not:

- Report anything known to be false.
- Manipulate images or sounds in any way that is misleading.
- Plagiarize.
- Present images or sounds that are reenacted without informing the public.

FAIRNESS

Professional electronic journalists should present the news fairly and impartially, placing primary value on significance and relevance.

Professional electronic journalists should:

- Treat all subjects of news coverage with respect and dignity showing particular compassion to victims of crime or tragedy.
- Exercise special care when children are involved in a story and give children greater privacy protection than adults.
- Seek to understand the diversity of their community and inform the public without bias or stereotype.
- Present a diversity of expressions, opinions and ideas in context
- Present analytical reporting based on professional perspective, not personal bias.
- Respect the right to a fair trial.

INTEGRITY

Professional electronic journalists should present the news with integrity and decency, avoiding real or perceived conflicts of interest, and respect the dignity and intelligence of the audience as well as the subjects of news.

Professional journalists should:

- Identify sources whenever possible. Confidential sources should be used only when it is clearly in the public interest to gather or convey impor-

tant information or when a person providing information might be
harmed.

- Journalists should keep all commitments to protect a confidential source.
- Clearly label opinion and commentary.
- Guard against extended coverage of events or individuals that fail to significantly advance a story, place the event in context, or add to the public knowledge.
- Refrain from contacting participants in violent situations while the situation is in progress.
- Use technological tools with skill and thoughtfulness, avoiding techniques that skew facts, distort reality, or sensationalize events.
- Use surreptitious newsgathering techniques, including hidden cameras or microphones, only if there is no other way to obtain stories of significant public importance and only if the technique is explained to the audience.
- Disseminate the private transmissions of other news organizations only with permission.

Professional electronic journalists should not:

- Pay news sources who have a vested interest in a story.
- Accept gifts, favors, or compensation from those who might seek to influence coverage.
- Engage in activities that may compromise their integrity or independence.

INDEPENDENCE

Professional electronic journalists should defend the independence of all journalists from those seeking influence or control over news content.

Professional electronic journalists should:

- Gather and report news without fear or favor, and vigorously resist undue influence from any outside forces, including advertisers, sources, story subjects, powerful individuals, and special interest groups.
- Resist those who would seek to buy or politically influence news content or who would seek to intimidate those who gather and disseminate the news.
- Determine news content solely through editorial judgment and not as the result of outside influence.

- Resist any self-interest or peer pressure that might erode journalistic duty and service to the public.
- Recognize that sponsorship of the news will not be used in any way to determine, restrict, or manipulate content.
- Refuse to allow the interests of ownership or management to influence news judgment and content inappropriately.
- Defend the rights of the free press for all journalists, recognizing that any professional or government licensing of journalists is a violation of that freedom.

ACCOUNTABILITY

Professional electronic journalists should recognize that they are accountable for their actions to the public, the profession, and themselves.

Professional electronic journalists should:

- Actively encourage adherence to these standards by all journalists and their employers.
- Respond to public concerns; investigate complaints and correct errors promptly and with as much prominence as the original report.
- Explain journalistic processes to the public, especially when practices spark questions or controversy.
- Recognize that professional electronic journalists are duty-bound to conduct themselves ethically.
- Refrain from ordering or encouraging courses of action that would force employees to commit an unethical act.
- Carefully listen to employees who raise ethical objections and create environments in which such objections and discussions are encouraged.
- Seek support for and provide opportunities to train employees in ethical decision-making.
  In meeting its responsibility to the profession of electronic journalism, RTNDA has created this code to identify important issues, to serve as a guide for its members, to facilitate self-scrutiny, and to shape future debate.

Reprinted by permission of the Radio-Television News Directors Association, 2002. The RTNDA Code of Ethics is available online, at http://www. rtnda.org/ethics/coe.shtml. RTNDA also has developed guidelines for reporters covering tough situations, such as interviewing and identifying juveniles

*and dealing with privacy issues. Those guidelines are available at http://
www.rtnda.org/ethics/ethicsguidelines.shtml.*

NATIONAL PRESS PHOTOGRAPHERS
ASSOCIATION CODE OF ETHICS

The National Press Photographers Association (NPPA), a professional society dedicated to the advancement of photojournalism, acknowledges concern and respect for the public's natural-law right to freedom in searching for the truth and the right to be informed truthfully and completely about public events and the world in which we live.

We believe that no report can be complete if it is not possible to enhance and clarify the meaning of words. We believe that pictures, whether used to depict news events as they actually happen, to illustrate news that has happened, or to help explain anything of public interest, are an indispensable means of keeping people accurately informed; that they help all people, young and old, to better understand any subject in the public domain.

Believing the foregoing we recognize and acknowledge that photojournalists should at all times maintain the highest standards of ethical conduct in serving the public interest. To that end the National Press Photographers Association sets forth the following code of ethics, which is subscribed to by all of its members.

1. The practice of photojournalism, both as a science and art, is worthy of the very best thought and effort of those who enter into it as a profession.
2. Photojournalism affords an opportunity to serve the public that is equaled by few other vocations, and all members of the profession should strive by example and influence to maintain high standards of ethical conduct free of mercenary considerations of any kind.
3. It is the individual responsibility of every photojournalist at all times to strive for pictures that report truthfully, honestly, and objectively.
4. As journalists, we believe that credibility is our greatest asset. In documentary photojournalism, it is wrong to alter the content of a photograph in any way (electronically or in the darkroom) that deceives the public. We believe the guidelines for fair and accurate reporting should be the criteria for judging what may be done electronically to a photograph.
5. Business promotion in its many forms is essential, but untrue statements

of any nature are not worthy of a professional photojournalist, and we condemn any such practice.

6. It is our duty to encourage and assist all members of our profession, individually and collectively, so that the quality of photojournalism may constantly be raised to higher standards.

7. It is the duty of every photojournalist to work to preserve all freedom-of-the-press rights recognized by law and to work to protect and expand freedom-of-access to all sources of news and visual information.

8. Our standards of business dealings, ambitions, and relations shall have in them a note of sympathy for our common humanity and shall always require us to take into consideration our highest duties as members of society. In every situation in our business life, in every responsibility that comes before us, our chief thought shall be to fulfill that responsibility and discharge that duty so that when each of us is finished, we shall have endeavored to lift the level of human ideals and achievement higher than we found it.

9. No code of ethics can prejudge every situation, thus common sense and good judgment are required in applying ethical principles.

Courtesy National Press Photographers Association, 2002. Reprinted with permission.

Appendix B: Canons, Standards, and Rules

ABA MODEL RULES OF PROFESSIONAL CONDUCT

RULE 3.6 TRIAL PUBLICITY

(a) A lawyer who is participating or has participated in the investigation or litigation of a matter shall not make an extrajudicial statement that the lawyer knows or reasonably should know will be disseminated by means of public communication and will have a substantial likelihood of materially prejudicing an adjudicative proceeding in the matter.

(b) Notwithstanding paragraph (a), a lawyer may state:

(1) the claim, offense or defense involved and, except when prohibited by law, the identity of the persons involved;

(2) information contained in a public record;

(3) that an investigation of a matter is in progress;

(4) the scheduling or result of any step in litigation;

(5) a request for assistance in obtaining evidence and information necessary thereto;

(6) a warning of danger concerning the behavior of a person involved, when there is reason to believe that there exists the likelihood of substantial harm to an individual or to the public interest; and

(7) in a criminal case, in addition to subparagraphs (1) through (6):

(i) the identity, residence, occupation and family status of the accused;

(ii) if the accused has not been apprehended, information necessary to aid in apprehension of that person;

    (iii) the fact, time and place of arrest; and
    (iv) the identity of investigating and arresting officers or agencies and
        the length of the investigation.

(c) Notwithstanding paragraph (a), a lawyer may make a statement that a reasonable lawyer would believe is required to protect a client from the substantial undue prejudicial effect of recent publicity not initiated by the lawyer or the lawyer's client. A statement made pursuant to this paragraph shall be limited to such information as is necessary to mitigate the recent adverse publicity.

(d) No lawyer associated in a firm or government agency with a lawyer subject to paragraph (a) shall make a statement prohibited by paragraph (a).

Comment

[1] It is difficult to strike a balance between protecting the right to a fair trial and safeguarding the right of free expression. Preserving the right to a fair trial necessarily entails some curtailment of the information that may be disseminated about a party prior to trial, particularly where trial by jury is involved. If there were no such limits, the result would be the practical nullification of the protective effect of the rules of forensic decorum and the exclusionary rules of evidence. On the other hand, there are vital social interests served by the free dissemination of information about events having legal consequences and about legal proceedings themselves. The public has a right to know about threats to its safety and measures aimed at assuring it security. It also has a legitimate interest in the conduct of judicial proceedings, particularly in matters of general public concern. Furthermore, the subject matter of legal proceedings is often of direct significance in debate and deliberation over questions of public policy.

[2] Special rules of confidentiality may validly govern proceedings in juvenile, domestic relations and mental disability proceedings, and perhaps other types of litigation. Rule 3.4(c) requires compliance with such rules.

[3] The Rule sets forth a basic general prohibition against a lawyer's making statements that the lawyer knows or should know will have a substantial likelihood of materially prejudicing an adjudicative proceeding. Recognizing that the public value of informed commentary is great and the likelihood of prejudice to a proceeding by the commentary of a lawyer who is not involved in the proceeding is small, the rule applies only to lawyers who are, or who have been involved in the investigation or litigation of a case, and their associates.

[4] Paragraph (b) identifies specific matters about which a lawyer's statements would not ordinarily be considered to present a substantial likelihood

of material prejudice, and should not in any event be considered prohibited by the general prohibition of paragraph (a). Paragraph (b) is not intended to be an exhaustive listing of the subjects upon which a lawyer may make a statement, but statements on other matters may be subject to paragraph (a).

[5] There are, on the other hand, certain subjects which are more likely than not to have a material prejudicial effect on a proceeding, particularly when they refer to a civil matter triable to a jury, a criminal matter, or any other proceeding that could result in incarceration. These subjects relate to:

(1) the character, credibility, reputation or criminal record of a party, suspect in a criminal investigation or witness, or the identity of a witness, or the expected testimony of a party or witness;

(2) in a criminal case or proceeding that could result in incarceration, the possibility of a plea of guilty to the offense or the existence or contents of any confession, admission, or statement given by a defendant or suspect or that person's refusal or failure to make a statement;

(3) the performance or results of any examination or test or the refusal or failure of a person to submit to an examination or test, or the identity or nature of physical evidence expected to be presented;

(4) any opinion as to the guilt or innocence of a defendant or suspect in a criminal case or preceding that could result in incarceration;

(5) information that the lawyer knows or reasonably should know is likely to be inadmissible as evidence in a trial and that would, if disclosed, create a substantial risk of prejudicing an impartial trial; or

(6) the fact that a defendant has been charged with a crime, unless there is included therein a statement explaining that the charge is merely an accusation and that the defendant is presumed innocent until and unless proven guilty.

[6] Another relevant factor in determining prejudice is the nature of the proceeding involved. Criminal jury trials will be most sensitive to extrajudicial speech. Civil trials may be less sensitive. Non-jury hearings and arbitration proceedings may be even less affected. The Rule will still place limitations on prejudicial comments in these cases, but the likelihood of prejudice may be different depending on the type of proceeding.

[7] Finally, extrajudicial statements that might otherwise raise a question under this Rule may be permissible when they are made in response to statements made publicly by another party, another party's lawyer, or third persons, where a reasonable lawyer would believe a public response is required in order to avoid prejudice to the lawyer's client. When prejudicial statements have been publicly made by others, responsive statements may have the salu-

tary effect of lessening any resulting adverse impact on the adjudicative proceeding. Such responsive statements should be limited to contain only such information as is necessary to mitigate undue prejudice created by the statements made by others.

[8] See Rule 3.8(f) for additional duties of prosecutors in connection with extrajudicial statements about criminal proceedings.

ABA Model Rules of Professional Conduct, 2002, Copyright 2002 American Bar Association. Reprinted by permission of the American Bar Association. Copies of the ABA Model Rules of Professional Conduct 2002 are available from Service Center, American Bar Association, 750 North Lake Shore Drive, Chicago, IL 60611–4497, 1–800–285–2221.

ABA STANDARDS FOR CRIMINAL JUSTICE, FAIR TRIAL, AND FREE PRESS

PART I. CONDUCT OF ATTORNEYS IN CRIMINAL CASES

Standard 8–1.1. Extrajudicial statements by attorneys

(a) A lawyer should not make or authorize the making of an extrajudicial statement that a reasonable person would expect to be disseminated by means of public communication if the lawyer knows or reasonably should know that it will have a substantial likelihood of prejudicing a criminal proceeding.

(b) Statements relating to the following matters are ordinarily likely to have a substantial likelihood of prejudicing a criminal proceeding:

(1) the prior criminal record (including arrests, indictments, or other charges of crime) of a suspect or defendant;

(2) the character or reputation of a suspect or defendant;

(3) the opinion of a lawyer on the guilt of the defendant, the merits of the case or the merits of the evidence in the case;

(4) the existence or contents of any confession, admission, or statement given by the accused, or the refusal or failure of the accused to make a statement;

(5) the performance of any examinations or tests, or the accused's refusal or failure to submit to an examination or test, or the identity or nature of physical evidence expected to be presented;

(6) the identity, expected testimony, criminal record or credibility of prospective witnesses;

(7) the possibility of a plea of guilty to the offense charged, or other disposition; and

(8) information which the lawyer knows or has reason to know would be inadmissible as evidence in a trial.

(c) Notwithstanding paragraphs (a) and (b), statements relating to the following matters may be made:

(1) the general nature of the charges against the accused, provided that there is included therein a statement explaining that the charge is merely an accusation and that the defendant is presumed innocent until and unless proven guilty;

(2) the general nature of the defense to the charges or to other public accusations against the accused, including that the accused has no prior criminal record;

(3) the name, age, residence, occupation and family status of the accused;

(4) information necessary to aid in the apprehension of the accused or to warn the public of any dangers that may exist;

(5) a request for assistance in obtaining evidence;

(6) the existence of an investigation in progress, including the general length and scope of the investigation, the charge or defense involved, and the identity of the investigating officer or agency;

(7) the facts and circumstances of an arrest, including the time and place, and the identity of the arresting officer or agency;

(8) the identity of the victim, where the release of that information is not otherwise prohibited by law or would not be harmful to the victim;

(9) information contained within a public record, without further comment; and

(10) the scheduling or result of any stage in the judicial process;

(d) Nothing in this standard is intended to preclude the formulation or application of more restrictive rules relating to the release of information about juvenile offenders, to preclude the holding of hearings or the lawful issuance of reports by legislative, administrative, or investigative bodies, to preclude any lawyer from replying to charges of misconduct that are publicly made against him or her, or to preclude or inhibit any lawyer from making otherwise permissible statement which serves to educate or inform the public concerning the operations of the criminal justice system.

*   *   *

PART III. CONDUCT OF JUDICIAL
PROCEEDINGS IN CRIMINAL CASES

Standard 8–3.1. Prohibition of direct restraints on media

Absent a clear and present danger to the fairness of a trial or other compelling interest, no rule of court or judicial order should be promulgated that prohibits representatives of the news media from broadcasting or publishing any information in their possession relating to a criminal case.

*Standard 8–3.2. Public access to judicial proceedings and
related documents and exhibits*

(a) In any criminal case, all judicial proceedings and related documents and exhibits, and any record made thereof, not otherwise required to remain confidential, should be accessible to the public, except as provided in section (b).
(b) (1) A court may issue a closure order to deny access to the public to specified portions of a judicial proceeding or related document or exhibit only after reasonable notice of and an opportunity to be heard on such proposed order has been provided to the parties and the public and the court thereafter enters findings that:

(A) unrestricted access would pose a substantial probability of harm to the fairness of the trial or other overriding interest which substantially outweighs the defendant's right to a public trial;
(B) the proposed order will effectively prevent the aforesaid harm; and
(C) there is no less restrictive alternative reasonably available to prevent the aforesaid harm.

(2) A proceeding to determine whether a closure order should issue may itself be closed only upon a prima facie showing of the findings required by Section b (1). In making the determination as to whether such a prima facie showing exists, the court should not require public disclosure of or access to the matter which is the subject of the closure proceeding itself and the court should accept submissions under seal, in camera or in any other manner designed to permit a party to make a prima facie showing without public disclosure of said matter.

(c) While a court may impose reasonable time, place and manner limitations on public access, such limitations should not operate as the functional equivalent of a closure order.

(d) For purposes of this Standard, the following definitions shall apply:

(1) "criminal case" shall include the period beginning with the filing of

an accusatory instrument against an accused and all appellate and collateral proceedings:

(2) "judicial proceeding" shall include all legal events that involve the exercise of judicial authority and materially affect the substantive or procedural interests of the parties, including courtroom proceedings, applications, motions, plea-acceptances, correspondence, arguments, hearings, trials and similar matters, but shall not include bench conferences or conferences on matters customarily conducted in chambers;

(3) "related documents and exhibits" shall include all writings, reports and objects, to which both sides have access, relevant to any judicial proceeding in the case which are made a matter of record in the proceeding;

(4) "public" shall include private individuals as well as representatives of the news media;

(5) "access" shall mean the most direct and immediate opportunity as is reasonably available to observe and examine for purposes of gathering and disseminating information;

(6) "closure order" shall mean any judicial order which denies public access.

*   *   *

Standard 8–3.6 *Conduct of the trial*

The following standards govern the conduct of a criminal trial when problems relating to the dissemination of potentially prejudicial materials are raised:

(a) Whenever appropriate, in view of the notoriety of a case or the number or conduct of news media representatives present at any judicial proceeding, the court should ensure the preservation of decorum by instructing those representatives and others as to the permissible use of the courtroom and other facilities of the court, the assignment of seats to news media representatives on an equitable basis, and other matters that may affect the conduct of the proceeding.

(b) Sequestration of the jury should be ordered if it is determined that the case is of such notoriety or the issues are of such a nature that, in the absence of sequestration, there is a substantial likelihood that highly prejudicial matters will come to the attention of the jurors. Either party may move for sequestration of the jury at the beginning of the trial, and, in appropriate circumstances, the court may order sequestration on its own motion. Whenever sequestration is ordered, the court, in advising the jury of the decision, should not disclose which party requested it. As an alternative to sequestration in cases where there is a significant threat of juror intimidation during or after the trial, the court may consider an order withholding public disclosure of jurors' names and addresses as long as that information is not otherwise required by law to be a matter of public record.

(c) Whenever appropriate, in light of the issues in the case or the notoriety of the case, the court should instruct jurors and court personnel not to make extrajudicial statements relating to the case or the issues in the case for dissemination by any means of public communication during the course of the trial and should caution parties and witnesses concerning the dangers of making an extrajudicial statement during trial. The court may also order sequestration of witnesses, prior to their appearance, when it appears likely that in the absence of sequestration they will be exposed to extrajudicial reports that may influence their testimony.

(d) In any case that appears likely to be of significant public interest, an admonition in substantially the following form should be given before the end of the first day if the jury is not sequestered:

> During the time you serve on this jury, there may appear in the newspapers or on radio or television reports concerning this case, and you may be tempted to read, listen to, or watch them. Please do not do so. Due process of law requires that the evidence to be considered by you in reaching your verdict meets certain standards; for example, a witness may testify about events personally seen or heard but not about matters told to the witness by others. Also, witnesses must be sworn to tell the truth and must be subjected to cross-examination. News reports about the case are not subject to these standards, and if you read, listen to, or watch these reports, you may be exposed to information which unduly favors one side and to which the other side is unable to respond. In fairness to both sides, therefore, it is essential that you comply with this instruction.

If the process of selecting a jury is a lengthy one, such an admonition should also be given to each juror as he or she is selected. At the end of each day of the trial, and at other recess periods if the court deems necessary, an admonition in substantially the following form should be given:

> For the reasons stated earlier in the trial, I must remind you not to read, listen to, or watch any news reports concerning this case while you are serving on this jury.

(e) If it is determined that material disseminated during the trial goes beyond the record on which the case is to be submitted to the jury and raises serious questions of possible prejudice, the court may on its own motion or should on the motion of either party question each juror, out of the presence of the others, about exposure to that material. The examination should take place at the presence of counsel, and an accurate record of the examination should be kept. The standard for excusing a juror who is challenged on the basis of such exposure should be the same as the standard of acceptability recommended in standard 8–3.5(b), except that a juror who has seen or heard reports of potentially prejudicial material should be excused if reference to the material in question at the trial itself would have required a mistrial to be declared.

*   *   *

Standard 8–3.8. *Broadcasting, Televising, Recording and Photographing Courtroom Proceedings*

A judge should prohibit broadcasting, televising, recording, or photographing in courtrooms and areas immediately adjacent thereto during sessions of court, or recesses between sessions, except that under rules prescribed by a supervising appellate court or other appropriate authority, a judge may authorize broadcasting, televising, recording and photographing of judicial proceedings in courtrooms and areas immediately adjacent thereto consistent with the right to a fair trial and subject to express conditions, limitations, and guidelines which allow such coverage in a manner that will be unobtrusive, will not distract or otherwise adversely affect witnesses or other trial participants, and will not otherwise interfere with the administration of justice.

ABA Standards for Criminal Justice: Fair Trial and Free Press, Third Edition. Copyright 1992 American Bar Association. Reprinted by permission of the American Bar Association, 2002.

CODE OF JUDICIAL CONDUCT CANON 3A

CANON 3: A JUDGE SHOULD PERFORM THE DUTIES OF THE OFFICE IMPARTIALLY AND DILIGENTLY

The judicial duties of a judge take precedence over all other activities. In performing the duties prescribed by law, the judge should adhere to the following standards:

A. Adjudicative Responsibilities

(1) A judge should be faithful to and maintain professional competence in the law, and should not be swayed by partisan interests, public clamor, or fear of criticism.

(2) A judge should hear and decide matters assigned, unless disqualified, and should maintain order and decorum in all judicial proceedings.

(3) A judge should be patient, dignified, respectful, and courteous to litigants, jurors, witnesses, lawyers, and others with whom the judge deals in an official capacity, and should require similar conduct of those subject to the judge's control, including lawyers to the extent consistent with their role in the adversary process.

(4) A judge should accord to every person who is legally interested in a proceeding, or the person's lawyer, full right to be heard according to law, and, except as authorized by law, neither initiate nor consider *ex parte* communications on the merits, or procedures affecting the merits of pending or impending proceeding. A judge may, however, obtain the advice of a disinterested expert on the law applicable to a proceeding before the judge if the judge gives notice to the parties of the person consulted and the substance of the advice, and affords the parties reasonable opportunity to respond. A judge may, with consent of the parties, confer separately with the parties and their counsel in an effort to mediate or settle pending matters.

(5) A judge should dispose promptly of the business of the court.

(6) A judge should avoid public comment on the merits of a pending or impending action, requiring similar restraint by court personnel subject to the judge's direction and control. This proscription does not extend to public statements made in the course of the judge's official duties, to the explanation of court procedures, or to a scholarly presentation made for purposes of legal education.

Code of Conduct for United States Judges. Courtesy Judicial Conference of the United States, 2002.

US DEPARTMENT OF JUSTICE 1–7.00
MEDIA RELATIONS

*   *   *

1–7.110 Interests Must Be Balanced

These guidelines recognize three principal interests that must be balanced: the right of the public to know; an individual's right to a fair trial; and the government's ability to effectively enforce the administration of justice.

*   *   *

1–7.112 Need for Free Press and Public Trial

[C]areful weight must be given in each case to the constitutional requirements of a free press and public trials as well as the right of the people in a constitutional democracy to have access to information about the conduct of law enforcement officers, prosecutors and courts, consistent with the individual rights of the accused. Further, recognition should be given to the needs of public safety, the apprehension of fugitives, and the rights of the public to be informed on matters that can affect enactment or enforcement of public laws or the development or change of public policy.

These principles must be evaluated in each case and must involve a fair degree of discretion and the exercise of sound judgment, as every possibility cannot be predicted and covered by written policy statement.

* * *

1–7.220 Designation of Media Representative

Each United States Attorney's Office and each field office of the various components of the Department shall designate one or more persons to act as a point of contact on matters pertaining to the media.

* * *

1–7.500 Release of Information Criminal and Civil Matters—Non-Disclosure

At no time shall any component or personnel of the Department of Justice furnish any statement or information that he or she knows or reasonably should know will have a substantial likelihood of materially prejudicing an adjudicative proceeding

1–7.520 Release of Information in Criminal and Civil Matters—Disclosable Information

Department personnel, subject to specific limitations imposed by law or court rule or order and consistent with the provisions of these guidelines, may make public the following information in any criminal case in which charges have been brought:

A. The defendant's name, age, residence, employment, marital status, and similar background information;

B. The substance of the charge, limited to that contained in the complaint, indictment, information, or other public documents;

C. The identity of the investigating and/or arresting agency and the length and scope of an investigation;

D. The circumstances immediately surrounding an arrest, including the time and place of arrest, resistance, pursuit, possession and use of weapons, and a description of physical items seized at the time of arrest. Any such disclosures shall not include subjective observations; and

E. In the interest of furthering law enforcement goals, the public policy significance of a case may be discussed by the appropriate United States Attorney or Assistant Attorney General. In civil cases, Department personnel may release similar identification material regarding defendants, the concerned government agency or program, a short statement of the claim, and the government's interest.

*   *   *

1–7.540 Disclosure of Information Concerning Person's Prior Criminal Record

Personnel of the Department shall not disseminate to the media any information concerning a defendant's or subject's prior criminal record, either during an investigation or at a trial. However, in certain extraordinary situations such as fugitive or in extradition cases, departmental personnel may confirm the identity of defendants or subject and offense or offenses. Where a prior conviction is an element of the current charge, such as in the case of a felon in possession of a firearm, departmental personnel may confirm the identity of the defendant and the general nature of the prior charge where such information is part of the public record in the case at issue.

1–7.550 Concerns of Prejudice

Because the release of certain types of information could tend to prejudice an adjudicative proceeding, Department personnel should refrain from making available the following:

A. Observations about a defendant's character;

B. Statements, admissions, confessions, or alibis attributable to a defendant, or the refusal or failure of the accused to make a statement;

C. Reference to investigative procedures, such as fingerprints, polygraph examinations, ballistic tests, or forensic services, including DNA testing, or the refusal by the defendant to submit to such tests or examinations;

D. Statements concerning the identity, testimony, or credibility of prospective witnesses;

E. Statements concerning evidence or argument in the case, whether or not it is anticipated that such evidence or argument will be used at trial;

F. Any opinion as to the defendant's guilt, or the possibility of a plea of guilty to the offense charged, or the possibility of a plea of a lesser offense.

1–7.600 Assisting the News Media

A. Other than by reason of a Court order, Department personnel shall not prevent the lawful efforts of the news media to photograph, tape, record or televise a sealed crime scene from outside the sealed perimeter.

B. In order to promote the aims of law enforcement, including the deterrence of criminal conduct and the enhancement of public confidence, Department personnel with the prior approval of the appropriate United States Attorney may assist the news media in photographing, taping, recording or televising a law enforcement activity. The United States Attorney shall consider whether such assistance would:

1. Unreasonably endanger any individual;
2. Prejudice the rights of any part or other person; and
3. Is not otherwise proscribed by law.

C. A news release should contain a statement explaining that the charge is merely an accusation and that the defendant is presumed innocent until and unless proven guilty.

D. In cases in which a search warrant or arrest warrant is to be executed, no advance information will be provided to the news media about actions to be taken by law enforcement personnel, nor shall media representatives be solicited or invited to be present. This prohibition will also apply to operations in preparation for the execution of warrants, and to any multi-agency action in which Department personnel participate.

E. Justice Department employees who obtain what may be evidence in any criminal or civil case or who make or obtain any photographic, sound or similar image thereof, in connection with a search or arrest warrant, may not disclose such material to the news media without the prior specific approval of the United States Attorney or Assistant Attorney General, who shall consider applicable regulations and policy, or upon a court order directing such production.

If news media representatives are present, Justice Department personnel may request them to withdraw voluntarily if their presence puts the operation or the safety of individuals in jeopardy. If the news media declines to withdraw, Department personnel should consider canceling the action if that is a practical alternative.

Exceptions to the above policy may be granted in extraordinary circumstances by the Office of Public Affairs.

US Attorney's Manual. Courtesy US Department of Justice, 2002

Appendix C: Guidelines for Coverage

GUIDELINES FOR THE PILOT PROGRAM ON PHOTOGRAPHING, RECORDING, AND BROADCASTING IN THE COURTROOM

1. General Provisions.

(a) Media coverage of federal court proceedings under the pilot program on cameras in the courtroom is permissible only in accordance with these guidelines.

(b) Reasonable advance notice is required from the media of a request to be present to broadcast, televise, record electronically, or take photographs at a particular session. In the absence of such notice, the presiding judicial officer may refuse to permit media coverage.

(c) A presiding judicial officer may refuse, limit, or terminate media coverage of an entire case, portions thereof, or testimony of particular witnesses, in the interests of justice to protect the rights of the parties, witnesses, and the dignity of the court; to assure the orderly conduct of the proceedings; or for any other reason considered necessary or appropriate by the presiding judicial officer.

(d) No direct public expense is to be incurred for equipment, wiring, or personnel needed to provide media coverage.

(e) Nothing in these guidelines shall prevent a court from placing additional restrictions, or prohibiting altogether, photographing, recording, or broadcasting in designated areas of the courthouse.

(f) These guidelines take effect July 1, 1991, and expire June 30, 1994.

2. Limitations.

(a) Coverage of criminal proceedings, both at the trial and appellate levels, is prohibited.

(b) There shall be no audio pickup or broadcast of conferences which occur in a court facility between attorneys and their clients, between co-counsel of a client, or between counsel and the presiding judicial officer, whether held in the courtroom or in chambers.

(c) No coverage of the jury, or of any juror or alternate juror, while in the jury box, in the courtroom, the jury deliberation room, or during recess, or while going to or from, the deliberation room at any time, shall be permitted. Coverage of the prospective jury during voir dire is also prohibited.

3. Equipment and Personnel.

(a) Not more than one television camera, operated by not more than one camera person, shall be permitted in any trial court proceeding. Not more than two television cameras, operated by not more than one camera person each, shall be permitted in any appellate court proceeding.

(b) Not more than one still photographer, utilizing not more than one camera and related equipment, shall be permitted in any proceeding in a trial or appellate court.

(c) If two or more media representatives apply to cover a proceeding, no such coverage may begin until all such representatives have agreed upon a pooling arrangement for their respective news media. Such pooling operations shall include the designation of operators, procedures for cost sharing, access to and dissemination of material, and selection of a pool representative if appropriate. The presiding judicial officer may not be called upon to mediate or resolve any dispute as to such arrangements.

(d) Equipment or clothing shall not bear the insignia or marking of a media agency. Camera operators shall wear appropriate business attire.

4. Sound and Light Criteria.

(a) Equipment shall not produce distracting sound or light. Signal lights or devices to show when equipment is operating shall not be visible. Motorized drives, moving lights, flash attachments, or sudden light changes shall not be used.

(b) Except as otherwise approved by the presiding judicial officer, existing courtroom sound and light systems shall be used without modification. Audio pickup for all media purposes shall be accomplished from existing audio systems present in the court facility, or from a television camera's built-in microphone. If no technically suitable audio system exists in the court facility, microphones and related wiring essential for media purposes shall be unobtrusive and shall be located in places designated in advance of any proceedings by the presiding judicial officer.

5. Location of Equipment and Personnel.

(a) The presiding judicial officer shall designate the location in the courtroom for the camera equipment and operators.

(b) During the proceedings, operating personnel shall not move about nor shall there be placement, movement, or removal of equipment, or the changing of film magazines, or lenses. All such activities shall take place each day before the proceeding begins, after it ends, or during a recess.

6. Compliance.

Any media representative who fails to comply with these guidelines shall be subject to appropriate sanction, as determined by the presiding judicial officer.

7. Review.

It is not intended that a grant or denial of media coverage be subject to appellate review insofar as it pertains to and arises under these guidelines, except as otherwise provided by law.

Approved by the Judicial Conference of the United States, September 1990. Revised June 1991.

CAMERAS IN THE COURTROOM

1. Authority
This policy is issued at the direction of the Judicial Conference of the United States. It was previously published as Canon 3A(7) in the *Code of Conduct for United States Judges.*
2. Scope
This policy is applicable to all United States district and appellate courts.
3. Policy
A judge may authorize broadcasting, televising, recording, or taking photographs in the courtroom and in adjacent areas during investiture, naturalization, or other ceremonial proceedings. A judge may authorize such activities

in the courtroom or adjacent areas during other proceedings, or recesses between other such proceedings, only:

(a) for the presentation of evidence;

(b) for the perpetuation of the record of the proceedings;

(c) for security purposes;

(d) for other purposes of judicial administration; or

(e) for the photographing, recording, or broadcasting of appellate arguments. When broadcasting, televising, recording, or photographing in the courtroom or adjacent areas is permitted, a judge should ensure that it is done in a manner that will be consistent with the rights of the parties, will not unduly distract participants in the proceeding, and will not otherwise interfere with the administration of justice.

The Judicial Conference Policy on Cameras in the Courtroom, reissued 10/14/97, Courtesy Administrative Office of the United States Courts, 2002.

Glossary

(Number in parentheses refers to chapter in which term is introduced.)

A

(3) acquittal (not guilty)—One of the possible **verdicts** in a criminal **trial**, based on the failure of the prosecution to meet the **burden of proof** of guilt. The prosecution may not appeal an **acquittal**. A journalist should report a **not guilty** verdict as an "**acquittal**" rather than describing the **verdict** as a **finding** of "innocent." Contrast: **conviction (guilty)**.

(4) actual (compensatory) damages—In a **civil action**, money that may be awarded to the victor to cover tangible, out-of-pocket losses caused by the injury. Compare: **punitive damages**.

(3) (admonish) admonition—A reprimand or warning by a judge to **trial** participants, particularly jurors, cautioning them to avoid exposure to press coverage of the case at hand in order to avoid prejudice.

(3) adversarial system—A description of the judicial process in the US in which one side is pitted against another with a judge or jury determining the victor.

(4) affidavit—A sworn statement made voluntarily, such as that made in a pre-trial **deposition** to be used in a **trial.**

(3) affirm—When an **appellate court** agrees with or upholds the decision of a lower court, and as a result, the lower court's decision remains in effect. Contrast: **reverse**.

(3) affirmative defense—In a **criminal action**, when a **defendant** does not deny the charge but argues police misconduct, self-defense, insanity, or some other circumstance in order to evade criminal responsibility. In a **civil action**, in order to avoid civil **liability**, when an **answer** to a **complaint** asserts the behavior under question was legally justified due to the statute of limitations or other grounds.

(4) alternative dispute resolution—Settlement of a civil case outside of the traditional court systems via **arbitration**, **mediation**, or a **summary jury trial**.

(4) *amicus curiae* (a-mee-kus ku-ree-ee, "friend of the court")—Outside parties interested in a lawsuit who may, with the permission of the court, **file** a **brief** supporting one of the **litigants** in the case. A reporter may contact an **amicus** for comments on the litigation. Compare: **intervenor**.

(4) answer—A **respondent**'s **pleading** in response to a **complaint** in a **civil action**: it denies in part or in whole the allegations of the **plaintiff**. A journalist should cover the **answer** with as much care as the **complaint**.

(3) appellant/appellee—The **defendant** in **criminal action** (or the losing party in a **civil action**) who appeals a decision to a higher court becomes the **appellant** in an appeal, and his name is listed first; the state in a **criminal action** (and the victor in a **civil action**) becomes the **appellee** in an appeal. **Appellants** may appeal (or "take an appeal of") not only the decision but also the penalty.

(3) appellate court—An intermediate or high court that has the power to review the **findings** of lower courts; the appeal is based on the grounds of a misapplication of the law rather than any factual **findings**. About half the states have intermediate **appellate courts**; the federal system has 13 **appellate courts** called **circuit courts**. Compare: **court of original jurisdiction** and **court of final resolution (supreme court)**.

(3) "approach the bench"—When a lawyer asks permission to speak to the judge during a **trial** outside the hearing of the jury to discuss an issue in private. Generally, no one except the opposing lawyer is allowed to listen in on the **bench conference**, or **sidebar**, and courtroom camera guidelines generally preclude any pickup—audio or video—of such discussions.

(4) arbitration—A type of **alternative dispute resolution** in which a neutral third party hears both sides and decides, with the decision usually binding. Such proceedings are rarely covered by the press. Compare: **mediation, summary jury trial**.

(3) arraignment—A preliminary hearing at which a criminal **suspect** is formally charged with a crime and officially enters a plea—**guilty, not guilty, no contest**, or (in some states) not guilty by reason of insanity or guilty and insane. In many courts, all the **arraignments** are scheduled on the same day in the same courtroom.

(3) arrest—Taking custody of a **suspect**. **Arrests** are generally made after a crime has been committed and a **warrant** describing **probable cause** has been issued.

(4) at issue—When the **pleadings** in a **civil action** reach a point where the parties have narrowed down the case to specific issues of disagreement; at this point the case is ready for the **trial** to begin.

B

(3) bail—Payment of money and/or a pledge of payment by a criminal **suspect** who, in exchange, is released from custody until his next scheduled court appearance. Often in the form of a bond for which the defendant puts up 10 percent and the bondsman puts up the rest. A suspect is "released on bail" or "released on bond."

(6) bailiff—The court official assigned to help the judge maintain order in the courtroom and to take charge of the jury, especially during deliberations.

(3) "Batson test"—Allegation during jury selection that a peremptory challenge is based on a potential juror's race: ruled unconstitutional in a 1986 US Supreme Court case; a subsequent case outlawed such challenges based merely on gender.

(3) **bench conference (sidebar)**—When lawyers for both sides in a case "**approach the bench**" outside the hearing of the jury to discuss an issue in private. Generally, no one else is allowed to listen in, and courtroom camera guidelines generally preclude any pickup—audio or video—of such discussions.

(4) **bench trial**—A case heard by a judge alone, without a jury. Contrast: **jury trial**.

(4) **best evidence**—Primary material such as an original of a document rather than secondary evidence such as a photocopy.

(3) **beyond a reasonable doubt**—The standard of proof of guilt in a **criminal action**, in which a juror must have an abiding conviction or be entirely convinced, more demanding than the standards in a **civil action**. Also, proof of such a convincing nature that you would act upon it without hesitation in the most important of your own affairs. Compare: **clear and convincing evidence** and **preponderance of evidence**.

(3) **bound over**—Describes a **suspect** held for **trial** or for appearance before a **grand jury**.

(3) **brief**—A written argument supporting one side in a case, **filed** by lawyers for each side.

(3) **burden of proof**—The standard or degree of belief regarding the facts in dispute that must be reached for a **finding** of guilt in a case: in a **criminal action** the **burden of proof** is guilt **beyond a reasonable doubt**; in a **civil action** the **burden of proof** might be **clear and convincing evidence** or a **preponderance of the evidence**.

C

(3) **capital crime**—A crime such as murder for which the punishment includes the possibility of the death penalty. Generally such cases require a **jury trial.**

(5) **caption**—The heading on a legal document such as a **pleading** or **motion** that gives names of **litigants**, the court identification number of the case, and the title of the action.

(4) **cause of action**—Legal basis on which a **civil complaint** is based.

(3) **challenge for cause**—To remove a prospective juror from the **venire** (jury pool) after questioning reveals some inherent unsuitability to serve on the jury. For instance, the juror may be related to one of the **trial** participants or in some other way is biased, or unable to be impartial. Usually each side in a **criminal action** has a limited number of such challenges. Contrast: **peremptory challenge**.

(3) **change of venue**—Moving a lawsuit to a different location within a **jurisdiction** due to the inability of a **defendant** to obtain a fair **trial** with impartial jurors in his home **jurisdiction** in a **criminal action**. In a **civil action** the change may be allowed in the interest of justice or for the convenience of the parties.

(3) **charge the jury (instruct the jury)**—When, in his final address to the jury, a judge presents guidelines to follow during the deliberations. A journalist should attend the **instruction** phase to enhance his understanding of the possible **verdicts** in the case.

(3) **circuit court**—The intermediate (**appellate**) court in the federal system. State courts in some jurisdictions also refer to their **trial** courts as **circuit** courts.

(3) **circumstantial evidence**—Evidence that is merely implied by a **witness's testimony**,

not based on the **witness**'s firsthand knowledge or personal observation. Compare: **direct evidence**.

(3) citation—An official notice to appear in court, often in regard to a **misdemeanor**; for instance a police officer may issue a traffic **citation**. A **citation** is generally regarded as a public record.

(3) civil action—One in which the **litigants** apply to the courts to resolve conflicts involving one party's claim of injury due to the actions of another. The **litigants** may be individuals, corporations or the government. Contrast: **criminal action**.

(8) class action—A **civil action** in which the **plaintiff** represents a group of people similarly affected by the injury claimed in the **complaint**.

(4) clear and convincing evidence—"Highly probable," a standard of proof of guilt required in certain **civil actions**. Less demanding than the standard in **criminal actions**—**beyond a reasonable doubt** ("abiding conviction") but more demanding than the standard in some other **civil actions**—**preponderance of evidence** ("more convincing weight of the argument").

(6) clerk of court—An employee of the court who keeps track of official **trial** documents such as evidence, administers oaths to **witnesses**, and generally assists in managing case flow.

(3) closing argument (summation)—After presentation of **testimony** for both sides in a **trial**, each side's final statements summing up the case and arguing for a decision in its favor. One of the crucial steps for journalists to cover in a **trial**.

(7) commutation—A reduction, generally by the governor of a state, of a **sentence** after **conviction** in a **criminal action**.

(4) compensatory (actual) damages—In a **civil action**, money that may be awarded to the victor to cover tangible, out-of-pocket losses caused by the injury. Compare: **punitive damages**.

(4) complaint (petition)—A document in a **civil action** charging one party with some wrong against another, the first step in the proceedings, generally available to the journalist in the **court clerk**'s office. In a **criminal action**, the charge—the **indictment** or **information**—may also be referred to as a **complaint**. The journalist should refer to information in a **complaint** as allegations, not facts.

(3) (concur)rence—In an **appellate court**, an opinion by a judge in which the judge agrees with the holding of the majority but has reasons different from those of the author of the majority decision. Contrast: **dissent**.

(3) concurrent (sentences)—For multiple crimes, such sentences combine the number of years in prison to run simultaneously. Contrast: **consecutive sentences**.

(3) consecutive (sentences)—For multiple crimes, such sentences add the number of years of the prison terms together to lengthen the sentence. Contrast: **concurrent sentences**.

(5) contempt—An order of a judge finding someone has violated an order of the court, embarrassed or hindered the court, or in some way obstructed the administration of justice. Journalists, for instance, risk being found in **contempt** for disobeying a **gag order**. "Direct" contempt is for actions in the presence of a judge, "indirect" contempt is for violation of a judge's order outside the courtroom. Possible penalties include a fine and/or a jail term.

(8) contingency—In **civil actions**, a method by which a lawyer, rather than collecting a set fee, receives a percentage of a monetary settlement.

(3) continuance—A delay or postponement in **trial** proceedings, generally granted by a judge in response to a request by one of the parties. A judge also may order a **continuance** in order to allow the effects of pre-trial publicity to diminish.

(4) contract—An agreement by two or more parties involving a promise to do or not to do something. Breach of **contract** may be the basis for a **civil action**.

(3) conviction (guilty)—A **finding** by the court that the **burden of proof** of guilt was met and the accused is **guilty** as charged. The **defendant** in a **criminal action** may attempt to appeal a **conviction**. A journalist should describe a **defendant** as **convicted** *of* a crime. Compare: **liability**. Contrast: **acquittal (not guilty)**.

(4) counterclaim—Possible reaction of a **respondent** in a **civil action** in which the **respondent** files a charge against the **plaintiff**.

(3) court of final resolution—The highest court in a judicial system, one with the power to **review** the actions of all lower courts in its **jurisdiction**. Generally referred to in most states and in the federal system as a **supreme court** ("Superior Court" in New York, "Supreme Judicial Court" in Maine and Massachusetts.) Compare: **appellate court** and **court of original jurisdiction.**

(3) court of original jurisdiction (trial court)—A lower or inferior court where a case begins, referred to as a **district court** in the federal system. Compare: **appellate court** and **court of final resolution (supreme court)**.

(6) court reporter—Person who records and prepares the official transcript of proceedings; this **record** is required for possible appeals.

(3) criminal action—One in which the government charges a **suspect** (who may be an individual or a corporation) with violating codes of behavior. Contrast: **civil action**.

(4) cross-appeal—In a **civil action**, a proceeding in which both parties appeal a **judgment**.

(3) cross-examination—Stage in a **trial** in which opposing lawyers question **witnesses** who have earlier offered **direct evidence**. Questioning is generally limited to topics covered in **direct** examination.

D

(4) damages—One possible goal of a **complaint** in a **civil action,** an award of money to compensate for injury done by one party to another.

(3) deadlocked (hung jury)—A jury unable to reach agreement on a **verdict**, with the vote usually required to be unanimous in a **criminal action** and often either three-fourths or five-sixths in a **civil action**.

(4) declaratory ruling—A judge's interpretation of a party's rights in a court case. It is the judge's opinion and does not order action by either party.

(3) defendant—An individual or corporation charged by the government in a **criminal action**.

(4) demurrer—Possible **pleading** of a **respondent** in a **civil action** in which the **respondent** states that even if the claims in the **complaint** are true, the **plaintiff** has no **cause of action** and the case should not proceed.

(3) *de novo*—("anew")—A re-trial of a case, usually ordered by a higher court on **remand**. The trial *de novo* is held just as if the original **trial** had never taken place.

(3) deposition—Sworn **testimony** of a **witness** outside of court, usually prior to **trial**, made in the presence of lawyers for both sides. **Depositions** generally do not become public record until (and unless) they are **filed** with the court. The **deposition** may substitute for **testimony** of a **witness** due to unavailability of the **witness** at the time of **trial**.

(3) determinate sentence—A fixed penalty set by **sentencing guidelines** that a judge in some cases is bound to follow after a **conviction** in a **criminal action**. Contrast: **indeterminate sentence**.

(3) direct evidence—Firsthand **testimony** of a **witness** by the party on whose behalf the **witness** was called, subject to **cross-examination** by opposing lawyers. Compare: **circumstantial evidence**.

(4) directed verdict—In a **civil action**, an order by a judge **finding** for one side or another based on the evidence, prior to the jury's deliberation, either on the judge's own initiative or based on a **motion** of a party. Compare: **judgment of acquittal (JOA)**.

(3) discovery—The pre-trial proceedings whereby lawyers for both sides may ask questions, **depose witnesses**, and gather evidence to be used in the **trial**. In federal courts and some states, discovery is reciprocal: the prosecution and defense must exchange information such as lists of witnesses to be called.

(3) dissent—In an **appellate court**, an opinion by a judge who disagrees with the holding of the majority. Contrast: **concurrence**.

(3) district attorney (DA, state's attorney)—The official prosecutor who represents the government in a **criminal action**. Usually elected, the **DA** (sometimes called the "county attorney") may be aided by numerous assistants (ADAs).

(3) district court—The **trial** court in the federal system, and in some states a **court of original jurisdiction**.

(4) diversity of citizenship—In a **civil action**, when the **litigants** are from different geographical areas, the matter of **jurisdiction**—which court will hear the case—is often the first issue of concern.

(3) docket—A calendar or schedule of legal proceedings in a court case, or (as a verb) to schedule legal proceedings.

(3) double jeopardy—The US Constitutional protection against a **defendant**'s being tried twice on the same charges and against multiple punishments for the same offense. **Double jeopardy** is not an issue if a **mistrial** ended an earlier **trial** or if someone's civil rights were violated, despite an earlier **acquittal** on **criminal** charges involving the same incident.

(3) due process—Safeguards that the system of justice under the US Constitution requires, such as a **defendant**'s right to a speedy **trial**.

E

(3) *en banc* ("on the bench")—An appeal heard by an entire group of judges rather than a subgroup or **panel**.

(4) enjoin—To order a party to act or not to act by means of an **injunction**.

(3) evidence in mitigation—During the penalty phase of a trial, argument for a lesser sentence due to circumstances surrounding the case.

(3) **exception for the record**—A type of formal **objection** to an action of the court based on a lawyer's **motion** that the court make an **overruled objection** part of the official **record** of the **trial** for use in appealing a **verdict**.

(3) **exclusionary hearing (suppression hearing)**—A pre-trial procedure by which a defense attorney in a **criminal action** asks the court to declare certain evidence **inadmissible** during the **trial** due to its being improperly obtained or because in some other way it violates the **rules of evidence**.

(3) *ex parte* ("**on one side only**")—Action such as contact by one **litigant** with a judge without notice to the other side, usually improper.

(3) **expert witness**—A **witness** who is qualified to offer opinions on certain matters due to special qualifications based on education or experience.

F

(3) **felony**—A major crime, ranging from grand larceny and burglary to assault, rape and murder, for which the penalty may be a state prison term of more than a year or even the death penalty. Contrast: **misdemeanor**.

(5) **file**—To enter officially documents with the court, generally via the office of the **clerk of the court**. Once **filed**, most documents become public record.

(3) **finding**—The result of deliberations of a judge or a jury.

(3) **first appearance (initial appearance)**—A court hearing at which a **suspect** who has been **arrested** is notified as to the possibility of **bail** and his right to legal counsel. Usually a **first appearance** is scheduled within twenty-four or forty-eight hours of **arrest**.

(3) **"fruit of the poisonous tree"**—**Tainted evidence**, obtained improperly and therefore **inadmissible** at **trial**.

G

(5) **"gag order" (restrictive order)**—A judge's order before or during a **trial** limiting public comments of **trial** participants. Prior restraints on the press are presumed unconstitutional, so a judge is generally required to hold a hearing before imposing a **restrictive order** on a journalist.

(3) **gain time**—Days subtracted from a prison **sentence** in a **criminal action** due to good behavior or other factors.

(3) **grand jury**—A panel of citizens (usually 12–23) who hear prosecutor's charges and **witnesses' testimony** in order to decide whether to charge a **suspect** with a crime. **Grand juries** also consider general issues such as corruption. Proceedings of **grand juries** are conducted in secret due to the unsubstantiated charges that may be discussed, and a journalist risks penalties for **contempt** if he is found to violate the secrecy of the **grand jury**. Compare: **petit jury**.

(3) **guilty (conviction)**—One of the possible **verdicts** in a **criminal action**, a **finding** by the court that the **burden of proof** of guilt was met and the accused is **guilty** as

charged. The **defendant** in a **criminal action** may attempt to appeal a **conviction.** Also, such a plea by a **defendant.** Contrast: **not guilty (acquittal).**

H

(7) *habeas corpus* **("you should have the body")**—A petition for a court order to bring a prisoner before the court to argue the legality of his imprisonment. A criminal **defendant** may also petition to **remove** a case from state court to federal court.

(3) **harmless error**—A minor mistake in procedure made by a **trial** court that an **appellate court** does not feel reached the status of grounds to **reverse** the lower court's **finding.** Contrast: **reversible error.**

(3) **hearsay**—Evidence **inadmissible** in a **criminal action** due to its being secondhand rather than direct observation of a **witness** who is testifying in a **trial.** There are several exceptions, such as spontaneous statements made at times of duress.

(3) **hung jury (deadlocked)**—A jury unable to reach agreement on a **verdict,** with the vote usually required to be unanimous in a **criminal action** and often either three-fourths or five-sixths in a **civil action.**

I

(3) **immunity**—The government's granting of protection to a **witness summoned** to appear before a **grand jury.** "Use" **immunity** means the testimony of the **witness** may not be used against him; "transactional" **immunity** means the **witness** may not be prosecuted at all in connection with the offense to which the **testimony** is related.

(3) **impanel**—To complete the process of jury selection in a jury **trial.** After the jury is sworn in, the **trial** officially begins.

(3) **impeach the witness**—To discredit a **witness,** for instance by comparing **testimony** given before the **trial** in a **deposition** with the same **witness's testimony** at the time of the **trial,** or by comparing the **testimony** of one **witness** with that of another.

(3) **inadmissible**—Evidence in a **trial** that a judge orders disallowed on grounds it does not meet legal standards or **rules of evidence.**

(3) *in camera* **("in chambers")**—Activity that takes place away from the jury and the public in the judge's private office.

(3) **indeterminate sentence**—One with a range of penalties (for example, a prison term of "twenty-five years to life") that a judge is bound by **sentencing guidelines** to follow in some **criminal actions.** Contrast: **determinate sentence.**

(3) **indictment ("true bill")**—A formal charge of a crime, generally a felony, issued by a **grand jury** after hearing from the **district attorney** and **witnesses** selected by the prosecution. The name of the target of the investigation will generally be written in all upper-case letters in the **caption:** the rest of the names are generally those of **witnesses** ordered to testify. The **indictment** is "handed up" to the judge. Contrast: **"no bill."** Compare: **presentment.**

(3) **information**—A process that in some states allows the **district attorney** to substitute

his own charge of a **suspect** with a crime rather than to require a **grand jury indict-ment.** Generally limited to **misdemeanors.**

(8) **"information and belief"**—A term used in **civil actions,** often in response to **inter-rogatories** and **requests for admission** in which a **witness** presents **testimony** that he has reason to believe is probably true.

(3) **initial appearance (first appearance)**—A court hearing at which a **suspect** who has been **arrested** is notified as to the possibility of **bail** and his right to legal counsel. Usually an **initial appearance** is scheduled within twenty-four or forty-eight hours of **arrest.**

(4) **injunction**—A court order to force or to halt some action, the **injunction** may be a goal of a **civil action.** A court may also issue a temporary **injunction** to halt some behavior while deliberating the legality of the proposed action. Compare: **tempo-rary restraining order (TRO).**

(3) *in limine* **("at the threshold")**—A motion *in limine* requests, prior to trial, that a court exclude certain evidence that might prejudice a jury.

(3) **instruct the jury (charge the jury)**—When, in his final address to the jury, a judge presents guidelines to follow during the deliberations. Instructions include factual questions to be answered and rules to follow. A journalist should attend the **instruc-tion** phase to enhance his understanding of the possible **verdicts** in the case.

(4) **interlocutory order**—A temporary order of the court, made in the midst of proceed-ings, not a final order.

(4) **interrogatories**—Sets of questions such as those issued by lawyers in a **civil action** prior to trial as part of the **discovery** process: they must be answered in writing under oath.

(4) **intervenor**—An outside party claiming an interest in a lawsuit who comes into the case in order to protect his claim. Compare: *amicus curiae.*

(3) **"invoke the rule"** (on exclusion of **witnesses**)—A request by a lawyer in a **criminal action** that **witnesses** be ordered to wait outside the courtroom during a **trial,** until they have testified, in order to avoid any "contamination" of their **testimony.**

J

(5) **jailbook ("police blotter")**—A chronological log listing names, addresses, dates, times and places of **arrests.** The **police blotter** is generally open to the public, although in some **jurisdictions** police have been known to keep a second, separate log unavailable to the public.

(3) **"jeopardy attaches"**—Once a jury is sworn in, a criminal trial officially begins, and at this point **jeopardy attaches** and the only way to halt proceedings is for the judge to declare a **mistrial.**

(3) **judgment n.o.v.** *(non obstante verdicto,* **"notwithstanding the verdict")**—The granting of a motion by a judge to find for one side or the other based on the evi-dence regardless of the jury's **verdict.**

(3) **judgment of acquittal (JOA)**—In a **criminal action,** the **finding** of a judge for one side or another based on the evidence prior to the jury's deliberation, either on the

judge's own initiative or on the **motion** of a party in a **criminal action**. Compare: **directed verdict**.

(4) jurisdiction—A court's authority to hear a case, including the geographic region in which a court has power. In a **civil action**, determining **jurisdiction** is often the first matter of consideration in a **complaint**.

(3) jury nullification—A situation in which a jury **acquits** a **defendant** despite overwhelming evidence of guilt.

(4) jury trial—A **trial** held before a group of qualified members of the community to determine the truth of a matter based on the evidence offered. Contrast: **bench trial**.

(3) justice—A judge in a high court (usually a **supreme court**). A high court will have an odd number of **justices** in order to avoid tie votes—for instance, the US Supreme Court has nine **justices**, one of whom serves as the Chief **Justice** of the United States.

L

(3) leading the witness—When a lawyer during examination of a witness at a **trial** improperly asks questions that strongly suggest the desired answer. The court will usually grant an opposing lawyer's **motion** to disallow evidence obtained by **leading the witness**.

(4) (liable) liability—In a **civil action**, a **finding** against a **litigant**. Compare: **conviction**.

(3) litigants—Parties to a case (the **plaintiff** as well as the **respondent** or **defendant**).

M

(3) magistrate—A court official found in the federal system and in some states, similar to a judge but with limited authority such as setting **bail** or hearing **misdemeanors**.

(8) mandamus ("we command")—An order issued by a higher court to a lower court directing some **judgment** be enforced.

(3) "McNaghten ("M'Naghten") rule"—A definition for insanity based on an 1843 case in which the **defendant** could not tell right from wrong. About half the states have replaced the test with that from the Model Penal Code that defines insanity as when the **defendant** lacks "substantial capacity" to "appreciate the criminality of his conduct" and to "confirm his conduct to the requirements of law."

(4) mediation—A type of **alternative dispute resolution** in which a mediator counsels both sides in an attempt to reach a compromise. Some **civil actions** in some **jurisdictions** mandate **mediation** prior to full court action, for instance in a child custody case. Compare: **arbitration, summary jury trial.**

(3) "Miranda Rule"—Based on a 1966 US Supreme Court case, the requirement that a **suspect** at the time of **arrest** be read notice of his Constitutional **due process** safeguards, such as the right to remain silent and the right to the services of a lawyer. Failure of an arresting office to do so may result in **inadmissibility** of evidence obtained.

(3) **misdemeanor**—A minor crime such as theft of something of low monetary value, for which the penalty may be a fine or a short jail term of one year or less. Contrast: **felony**.

(3) **mistrial**—Invalidation of a **trial** due to a **hung jury** or due to some interference with **due process**. A new **trial** may be ordered without invoking **double jeopardy** after a **mistrial** has been declared. The press may cause a **mistrial** by violating a **gag order**, by contacting a juror, or by in any way interfering with the **due process** rights of the **defendant**.

(3) **moot**—A legal issue not open for consideration, including matters already settled.

(3) **motion**—A procedure by which a litigant asks the court for a decision relating to the case.

(4) **motion to dismiss**—A request by a **respondent** in a **civil action** for the court to declare the **plaintiff** has not presented sufficient evidence for a **finding** in his favor, or a **complaint** does not merit further court action, or the issue is already settled, and calls for an end to the proceedings.

N

(3) **negotiated settlement ("plea bargain")**—An agreement reached in a **criminal action** by lawyers for both sides and approved by the judge in which, in return for pleading **guilty** to a lesser crime than that with which he was originally charged, a **defendant** receives a reduced sentence. More than two-thirds of criminal proceedings end up in **plea bargains** rather than **trials**. The press has little access to the actual negotiations, but the judge must approve the agreement in open court.

(3) **"no bill"**—A **finding** of a **grand jury** of insufficient evidence to charge a **suspect** with a crime. Contrast: **indictment ("true bill")**. Compare: **presentment**.

(3) *nolle prosequi* (**nol-a pros-e-kwee, "will no further prosecute"**)—A decision by the prosecutor in a **criminal action** to drop the charges before a case has reached the **trial** stage. About a third of all criminal charges in the US today end up being dropped.

(3) *nolo contendere* (*"nolo"*) (**no-lo kon-ten-de-ray, "I will not contest it," "no contest"**)—One of the possible pleas that a **suspect** in a **criminal action** may select at his **arraignment**. The plea, which must be approved by the judge, allows the **defendant** to accept the penalty for the crimes with which he is charged, without formally admitting guilt and without facing future **civil action** in regard to the incident

(3) **not guilty (acquittal)**—One of the possible **verdicts** in a criminal **trial**, based on the failure of the prosecution to meet the **burden of proof** of guilt. The prosecution may not appeal an **acquittal**. A journalist should report a **not guilty verdict** as an "acquittal" rather than describing the **verdict** as a **finding** of "innocent." Also, a **defendant** may plead **not guilty** to a criminal charge, thus necessitating a **trial**. Contrast: **guilty (conviction)**.

(3) **notice of appeal**—Document that must be **filed** in a **timely** fashion by a **convicted defendant** in a **criminal case** (or the losing **litigant** in a **civil case**) stating the legal grounds on which the **defendant** claims a higher court should reconsider the decision.

O

(3) (object)ion—When a lawyer for either side in a court case asks the court to disallow evidence or some legal procedure on the grounds it is not legally proper—for instance it is evidence that was improperly obtained or that otherwise violates the **rules of evidence**. A judge may **overrule** (disregard) or **sustain** (apply) an **objection**. In an (improper) **"speaking objection"** a lawyer tries to work in a hint to the **witness** as to how to answer the question in case the **objection** is **overruled**.

(3) of counsel—A lawyer who assists in a case although he does not play a primary role as an attorney of record.

(3) offer of proof—When, in the absence of the jury during a **trial**, a lawyer describes evidence that would have been heard if the court had not **sustained** an **objection**. The **offer** becomes part of the official **record** in case there is an appeal of the **verdict**.

(3) opening statement—Made by lawyers for each side in a **trial** after the jury is **impaneled**. **Opening statements** are not evidence and should not argue for or against a position but should describe the upcoming case and outline the facts to be considered. Generally, prosecutors must make **opening statements**, while they are optional for the defense. Journalists are cautioned, first, to report on **opening statements**, a crucial part of the case, and second, not to call them "opening arguments."

(3) overrule—When a judge allows certain actions or admits certain evidence in a case despite a lawyer's **objection** that it violates the **rules of evidence** or is otherwise improper. Also, the **finding** of a lower court may be **overruled** by a higher court if the higher court rejects the decision of the lower court. Contrast: **sustain**.

P

(3) panel (judges)—A selected group of judges who hear an appeal. For instance, often a **panel** of three judges out of five on a court will consider an individual appeal.

(3) panel (jury)—Groups of prospective jurors who are questioned prior to a **trial** during *voir dire* (jury selection) in order to determine their suitability to serve.

(7) pardon—Elimination of or setting aside of a **sentence** after a **conviction** in a **criminal action**, thereby releasing the person from further punishment. The President usually issues **pardons** in federal cases, while governors issue **pardons** in state cases.

(7) parole—Release of a prisoner after a hearing; the **sentence** remains although it is no longer in effect.

(3) per curium ("by the court")—A decision by an **appellate court** that is issued without any explanation by the judges of their grounds for the holding.

(3) peremptory challenge—To remove a prospective juror from the **venire** (jury pool) for unstated reasons. Each side in a **criminal action** has a limited number of **peremptory challenges**. Contrast: **challenge for cause**.

(3) perjury—A false statement made under oath in any judicial proceeding by any participant.

(3) petit jury—A six- or twelve-member jury that meets in the courtroom and hears evidence in a **trial**. Compare: **grand jury**.

(4) petition (complaint)—A document in a **civil action** charging one party with some wrong against another, the first step in proceedings. Generally available to the journalist in the **court clerk**'s office. May also apply to any written application to the court requesting some action.

(3) plaintiff—In a lawsuit, the party who brings a case into court. In a **criminal action**, the government charges the **defendant** with violating the laws of society; in a **civil action**, the **plaintiff** files a **complaint** charging some injury by a **respondent,** and either party may be an individual, a corporation, or the government.

(3) "plea bargain" (negotiated settlement)—An agreement reached in a **criminal action** by lawyers for both sides and approved by the judge in which, in return for pleading **guilty** to a lesser crime than that which he was originally charged, a **defendant** receives a reduced sentence. More than two-thirds of criminal proceedings end up in **plea bargains** rather than **trials**. The press has little access to the actual negotiations, but the judge must approve the agreement in open court.

(4) pleadings—The exchange of documents **filed** with the court. In a **civil action,** including the **complaint**, the **answer**, possible **demurrers**, **counterclaims**, and replies.

(5) "police blotter" (jailbook)—A chronological log listing names, addresses, dates, times and places of **arrests**. The **police blotter** is generally open to the public, although in some **jurisdictions** police have been known to keep a second, separate log unavailable to the public.

(3) poll (the jury)—A request by one side in a court case, usually the losing side, to have each juror stand and declare aloud his vote on the **verdict** before the jury is dismissed.

(3) preliminary hearing—In **felony** cases that did not originate with a **grand jury**, a hearing in which a judge decides whether enough evidence exists to charge a **suspect** with a crime. In some **jurisdictions**, the **preliminary hearing** is combined with the **arraignment**.

(3) "prepare" (a witness)—To rehearse questions and answers with a **witness** by a lawyer before the **witness** actually testifies in court.

(4) preponderance of evidence—A standard of proof of guilt required in some **civil actions**, based on a "more convincing weight of the argument," at least 51 percent. Less demanding than the standard in **criminal actions—beyond a reasonable doubt** ("abiding conviction") and also less demanding than the standard in some other **civil actions—clear and convincing evidence** ("highly probable").

(6) presentment—A report by a **grand jury** on a general issue such as corruption, released after convening, without any official **finding**. Compare: **indictment ("true bill")** and **"no bill."**

(3) presumption of innocence—Assumption under the Sixth Amendment of the US Constitution that every **defendant** in a **criminal action** is entitled to protections that assume he is innocent of any wrongdoing until he is declared **guilty** after **due process** of law. A journalist has to remain wary not to imply guilt of any **defendant** prior to a court's **verdict**.

(3) probable cause—Good reason to believe certain facts, such as that a **suspect** has committed a crime; the basis for a court's issuing a **warrant** for search for and/or **arrest** of a **suspect** or for holding a **defendant** prior to **trial**.

(3) probation—The decision of a court to **suspend** a **sentence** after **conviction**, ordering the **defendant** to meet certain conditions such as community service. If the conditions are not met, the **defendant** will return to serve out the **sentence**.

(3) *pro bono* ("for the good")—For no cost, describing lawyers who may volunteer or be assigned by the court to represent indigent **litigants**, particularly **defendants** in **criminal actions** in **jurisdictions** with no **public defender.**

(3) proffer—Offer of evidence to a judge for consideration of whether it will be admissible at trial.

(3) pro se ("in one's own behalf")—Representing oneself in a court case, presenting the case without a lawyer.

(3) public defender—A lawyer who represents an indigent **litigant**, particularly a **defendant** in a **criminal action**, with his services paid for by the state.

(4) punitive damages—In a **civil action**, an award designed to punish the **respondent** for wrongdoing. In many cases, high **punitive damages** awarded by a jury are subsequently reduced by a judge or **appellate court**. Compare: **compensatory (actual) damages**.

Q

(3) qualifying the jury—The questioning of jurors during *voir dire* as to whether they would be able to vote to impose a death penalty in a case involving a **capital crime** if the **defendant** were to be **convicted**.

(3) quash—An order of a court to cancel or void a **summons** or a **subpoena** for **testimony** or evidence or an **indictment** due to some failure to follow procedure or to meet legal standards.

R

(3) rebuttal witness—During a **trial**, a **witness** who is called by a lawyer who has already **rested** his case to refute the **testimony** of a **witness** for the other side.

(3) record—Written transcripts of a court proceeding, the only official version, made by a **court reporter** and often used as a basis for subsequent appeals of a court's action. The **record** includes **pleadings**, evidence, and exhibits. Some courts are experimenting with the use of audio/video to create the official **record**.

(5) redact—To remove certain information from an official document, such as the names of police informants or references by one joint **defendant** to another in a confession.

(3) "re-cross"—When a lawyer **cross-examines** for a second time a **witness** who has just been subjected to **re-direct** by the lawyer who called the **witness** to **testify** in the first place.

(3) "re-direct"—When a lawyer re-examines his own **witness** after the **witness** has been **cross-examined** by the opposing lawyer.

(3) rejoinder—When, during the second half of a **trial**, a **witness** presents **testimony** to refute the **testimony** of a **rebuttal witness**.

(3) released on recognizance (ROR)—When a court allows a **defendant** to remain free while awaiting future court actions without having to pay **bail**, based on the person's "recognition" or reputation and standing in the community.

(3) remand ("send back")—An order by an **appellate court** for a lower court to take some further action in a case.

(7) remove—To transfer a case from one **jurisdiction** to another, for example from state court to federal court.

(4) reply—A possible response of a **plaintiff** in a **civil action** to a **respondent**'s **answer** or **counterclaim**.

(4) requests for admission—During the **discovery** process, written responses to charges in a **complaint**: each charge must be admitted or denied.

(4) *res judicata* (riz jude-u-kata, "thing adjudicated")—A possible **answer** to a **complaint** in a **civil action**, suggesting that a matter already settled need not be re-opened.

(3) respondent—The party against whom a **complaint** is filed in a **civil action**; the **respondent** may be an individual, a corporation, or the government. In an appeal, the party against whom the appeal is **filed** is the **respondent**.

(3) rest (a case)—During a **trial**, when each side in turn announces it has finished presenting **witnesses** and evidence. The prosecution is the first to **rest**.

(5) restrictive order ("gag order")—A judge's order before or during a **trial** limiting public comments of **trial** participants. Prior restraints on the press are presumed unconstitutional, so a judge is generally required to hold a hearing before imposing a **restrictive order** on a journalist.

(5) return—The notes regarding an action such as that taken under a search or **arrest warrant**. The **return** should be made available to the press as part of the case file.

(3) reverse—When an **appellate court** orders the decision of a lower court overturned due to some flaw of Constitutional dimensions in the procedure followed by the lower court. A **reversal** may include a **remand**. Contrast: **affirm.**

(3) reversible error—A major mistake in procedure made by a **trial** court that an **appellate court** feels is serious (prejudicial) enough to require setting aside the opinion of the lower court and possibly reconsidering the issue. Contrast: **harmless error**.

(3) review—To reexamine judicially the actions of a lower court by a higher court.

(3) rules of evidence—Official standards that must be met in order for a court to allow evidence to be introduced (declared admissible) during a **trial**.

S

(3) sentence—Punishment determined by a judge in a **criminal action** after a **conviction** of guilt (in some **jurisdictions** based on a jury's recommendation).

(3) sentencing guidelines—Rules in federal court and in many states requiring a judge remain within a range of **sentences** for **convictions** on various crimes in an effort to insure uniformity and fairness.

(3) sequester—To isolate the jury during the course of a **criminal trial** in order to protect the jurors from possible prejudicial publicity.

(3) serve—To officially carry out a **warrant** or **summons** requiring the taking of some action ordered by the court.

(3) set aside—An order by a court to override the actions of a lower court.

(4) settlement—Analogous to a **plea bargain** in a **criminal action**, the **settlement** in a **civil action** results when the **litigants** from both sides agree to terms outside the court and then present their agreement to the judge for approval. As with **criminal actions**, most **civil actions** are **settled** prior to **trial**.

(3) sidebar (bench conference)—When lawyers for both sides in a case "**approach the bench**" outside the hearing of the jury to discuss an issue in private. Generally, no one else is allowed to listen in, and courtroom camera guidelines generally preclude any pickup—audio or video—of such discussions.

(3) "speaking objection"—In an improper "**speaking objection**" a lawyer tries to work in a hint to the **witness** as to how to answer the question in case the **objection** is **overruled**

(4) special appearance—In a **civil action**, the **filing** of a notice that a **respondent** acknowledges receipt of a **complaint** but contends the court has no **jurisdiction** in the case. It is necessary in order to avoid losing by default.

(4) standing—The right of a party to become a **litigant** in a **civil action**.

(3) state's attorney (district attorney)—The official prosecutor who represents the government in a **criminal action**. Usually elected, the **state's attorney** (sometimes called the "county attorney") may be aided by numerous assistants (ADAs).

(7) stay—To temporarily halt or suspend proceedings, usually by means of an **injunction**.

(3) stipulation—An agreement on certain facts by both sides prior to a **trial**.

(3) strike—During *voir dire* (jury selection), to dismiss a prospective juror from sitting on the panel due either to a stated reason (**challenge for cause**) or for no stated reason (**peremptory challenge**).

(3) subpoena ("under penalty")—An official order to appear in court. A journalist might be **subpoenaed** to appear in court to **testify** regarding his sources for a story and is subject to being found in **contempt** for failure to comply.

(5) subpoena *duces tecum* (du-sez te-kum, "you must take it with you")—An official order to appear in court and to bring certain documents with you. A journalist might be **subpoenaed** to appear in court to **testify** and to bring with him such material as notes or audio or videotapes.

(4) summary judgment—In a **civil action**, when the parties agree on the facts but one side feels entitled to prevail as a matter of law and asks the court for a **summary judgment**, a ruling in his favor without a trial.

(4) summary jury trial—A type of **alternative dispute resolution** in which the parties present facts to a mock jury whose verdict helps them determine terms of settlement. Compare: **arbitration, mediation**.

(3) summation (closing argument)—After presentation of **testimony** for both sides in a **trial**, each side's final statements summing up the case and arguing for a favorable decision. One of the crucial steps for journalists to cover in a **trial**.

(3) summons—An official notification of legal action, such as the **filing** of a **complaint** or a **subpoena**.

(3) suppression hearing (exclusionary hearing)—A pre-trial procedure by which a defense attorney in a **criminal action** asks the court to declare certain evidence inadmissible during the **trial** due to its being improperly obtained or because in some other way it violates the **rules of evidence**.

(3) supreme court (court of final resolution)—The highest court in a judicial system, one with the power to **review** the actions of all lower courts in its **jurisdiction**. Generally referred to in most states and in the federal system as a **supreme court**. ("Superior Court" in New York, "Supreme Judicial Court" in Maine and Massachusetts). Compare: **appellate court** and **court of original jurisdiction.**

(3) suspect—A person named on a **warrant** as one for whom **probable cause** to believe he has committed a crime exists. A **suspect** becomes a **defendant** only after he is **indicted** and/or **arraigned**.

(3) suspended sentence—A court decision to hold a penalty in abeyance due to mitigating circumstances despite **conviction**.

(3) sustain—When a judge upholds a lawyer's **objection** to admission of evidence or some action in a case, agreeing that it violates **rules of evidence** or proper court procedure. Contrast: **overrule.**

T

(3) tainted evidence—Evidence **inadmissible** in a **criminal action** by virtue of its being in some way faulty, such as improperly obtained, or in any way violative of the **rules of evidence**.

(3) tamper (with the jury)—To interfere in any way with the secrecy of deliberations or the need for the jury to remain impartial: it is a criminal offense. A journalist who **tampers** with a jury may be found in **contempt** and possibly cause a **mistrial**.

(4) temporary restraining order—An order prohibiting a certain action, it may be granted by a judge without a hearing. Compare: **injunction.**

(3) testimony—Official statements made under oath by **witnesses** in a judicial proceeding.

(3) timely—Meeting a legal deadline. For instance, motions to appeal must be filed in a **timely** fashion in order to be valid.

(4) tort—In a **civil action**, a wrong inflicted by one party upon another, and the grounds for the **complaint**.

(3) trial—A court proceeding in which the facts are determined either by a judge alone (a **bench trial**) or by a judge and a jury (a **jury trial**) in a **trial** court, or **court of original jurisdiction**.

(3) "true bill" (indictment)—A formal charge of a crime, issued by a **grand jury** after hearing from the **district attorney** and **witnesses** selected by the prosecution. Contrast: **"no bill."** Compare: **presentment.**

U

(4) US attorney—The prosecutor in a federal court, analogous to the **district attorney (DA)** or **state's attorney** in state court. However, **US attorneys** are generally appointed in a highly partisan process while **DA**s are generally elected.

V

(3) vacate—To annul, set aside, cancel an order.

(3) *venire* (ve-ni-ree "to come")—The pool of potential jurors in a **trial**, selected in most states from voter registration lists or a combination of voter registration lists, tax rolls, and driver license registration lists. A journalist should be cautious in talking to members of the **venire** to avoid charges of jury **tampering**.

(3) verdict ("true declaration")—The decision after a jury deliberates, the finding of **guilt** or **acquittal** of the **defendant** in a **criminal action**, or of **liability** or lack thereof in a **civil action.**

(6) victim advocate—In some **jurisdictions**, a court employee, or more often a volunteer, who attends the **trial**. The **victim advocate** is dedicated to protecting the right of victims and their families.

(3) *voir dire* (vwar deer, "to speak the truth")—Pre-trial process of jury selection during which members of the **venire** (jury pool) are questioned to determine their suitability to serve. Case law supports public access to the *voir dire*.

W

(3) warrant—An official order issued by a judge, such as a **warrant** for the search for and **arrest** of a **suspect** due to a finding of **probable cause** that he is suspected of a crime.

(4) "with prejudice"—When a case is dismissed and may not be re-filed.

(3) witness—A person who **testifies** under oath in a judicial proceeding.

(3) writ of *certiorari* (ser-she-o-ra-ree, "to be informed of")—A order by the US Supreme Court granting a petition to consider a case.

Selected Bibliography

"About Court TV." www.courttv.com (accessed 2002).

"Actions Taken against Judges for Talking to Media Contested." (RCFP) *The News Media and the Law* (Fall 1998): 16–17.

Alexander, S. L. "Cameras in the Courtroom: A Case Study." *Judicature* 74:6 (April–May 1991): 307–313.

———. "Curious History: The ABA Code of Judicial Ethics Canon 35." *Mass Comm Review* 18:3 (1991): 31–37ff.

———. "The Impact of *California v Simpson* on Cameras in the Courtroom." *Judicature* 79:4 (January–February 1996): 169–172.

———. "Mischievous Potentialities: *A Case Study of Courtroom Camera Guidelines.*" PhD dissertation, University of Florida, 1990.

———. "A Reality Check on Court/Media Relations." *Judicature* 84:3 (November–December 2000): 146–149.

———. "Their Day in Court." Society of Professional Journalists *Quill* (June 2000): 10–13.

———. "Trials of the Century: *US v Edwin Edwards* 2000." *Louisiana State Bar Association Journal*, 48:4 (December 2000): 290–294.

American Bar Association. *Facts about the American Judicial System.* Chicago: 1999, available at www.abanet.org (accessed 2002).

———. *Fair Trial/Free Press Voluntary Agreements.* Chicago: ABA, 1974.

———. *A Journalist's Guide to Civil Procedure.* Chicago: ABA, 1993, videocassette.

———. *A Journalist's Guide to Federal Criminal Procedure.* Chicago: ABA, 1989, videocassette.

———. *A Journalist's Primer on Civil Procedure.* Chicago: ABA, 1993.

———. *A Journalist's Primer on Federal Criminal Procedure.* Chicago: ABA, 1988.

———. *Law and the Courts.* Chicago: ABA, 1987.

———. *Model Rules of Professional Conduct and Code of Judicial Conduct.* Chicago: ABA, 1989.

———. *The Rights of Fair Trial and Free Press: The American Bar Association Standards: An Information Manual for the Bar, News Media, Law Enforcement Officials and Courts.* Chicago: ABA, 1981.

————. *Standards for Criminal Justice Fair Trial and Free Press.* 3rd ed. Washington, DC: ABA, 1992.

American Bar Association and the National Conference of Lawyers and Representatives of the Media. *The Reporter's Key: Rights of Fair Trial and Free Press.* Chicago: ABA, 1994.

American Board of Trial Advocates. "Accuracy in Legal Journalism Reporting Code," at www.abota.org (accessed 2002).

American Society of Newspaper Editors/American Newspaper Publishers Associationoo Foundation. *Free Press and Fair Trial.* Washington, DC: ASNE/ANPA, 1982.

Arnold, Hon. Richard. In "Justice by the Consent of the Governed: Interview with Judge Richard S. Arnold and Judge Gilbert S. Merritt." *Media Studies Journal: Covering the Courts* 12:1 (Winter 1998): 80–91.

The Associated Press Stylebook and Briefing on Media Law. Edited by Norm Goldstein. Cambridge, Mass.: Perseus, 2000.

Barber, Susanna. *News Cameras in the Courtroom: A Free Press–Fair Trial Debate.* Norwood, N.J.: Ablex Publishing Corp., 1987.

Bennett, Robert. "Press Advocacy and the High-Profile Client." *Loyola of Los Angeles Law Review* 30:7 (November 1996): 13–20.

Black's Law Dictionary. 6th ed. St. Paul, Minn.: West Publishing, 1990.

Boland, Robert, and Kennard Strutin. "Media Relations for the Criminal Defense Lawyer." *The Practical Litigator* (July 1993): 59–70.

Boles, Nancy, and Katherine Heaviside. "When a Reporter Calls." American Bar Association *ABA Journal* 73 (1 June 1987): 90–94.

Bosco, Joseph. *A Problem of Evidence: How the Prosecution Freed OJ Simpson.* New York: William Morrow, 1996.

Bresler, Ken. "How to Handle Reporters." *The Florida Bar Journal* (November 1988): 23–24.

Buckman, Robert. "I Feel Stronger." Society of Professional Journalists *Quill* (January–February 2002): 18–22.

Bunker, Matthew. *Justice and the Media: Reconciling Fair Trials and a Free Press.* Mahwah, N.J.: Lawrence Erlbaum, 1997.

Campbell, Douglas. *Free Press v Fair Trial: Supreme Court Decisions Since 1807.* Westport, Conn.: Praeger, 1994.

Caplan, Lincoln. "The Failure (and Promise) of Legal Journalism." In *Postmortem, The OJ Simpson Case: Justice Confronts Race, Domestic Violence, Lawyers, Money, and the Media,* 199–207, edited by Jeffrey Abramson. New York: Basic Books, 1996.

Carlton, A. P. "ABA Strives to Save a Constitutional, Impartial Judiciary." *(Sacramento) Daily Recorder,* 20 September 2000.

"Cloaked in Secrecy, Public Rights Suffer in Westfield Case." *San Diego Union-Tribune,* 12 May 2002, sec. G–2.

Cohen, Andrew. "Lessons from the Timothy McVeigh Trial II." *Media Studies Journal: Covering the Courts* 12:1 (Winter 1998): 14–17.

Cohn, Marjorie, and David Dow. *Cameras in the Courtroom: TV and the Pursuit of Justice.* Jefferson, N.C.: McFarland and Company, 1998.

Colby, William. "When the Media Calls." *The Kansas Journal of Law and Public Policy* (Spring 1995): 77–80.

Cooper, A. Lee. "Don't Get Trampled by Media Circus.*"* American Bar Association *ABA Journal* (February 1997): 8.

Costa, Joseph. "Cameras in Courtrooms: A Position Paper." Manuscript, Ball State University Journalism/Public Relations Research Center, 1980.

Court TV. "Facts and Opinions About Cameras in Courtrooms." Manuscript, Court TV, July 1995.

"Court TV Gains Approval." *Broadcasting and Cable*, 17 July 2000, 20–24.

Coyle, Pamela. "Court Records." Manuscript, Investigative Reporters and Editors National Conference, New Orleans, Louisiana, 5 June 1998.

DeBenedictus, Don. "The National Verdict." *ABA Journal* (October 1994): 52–55.

Denniston, Lyle. "How to Deal With Journalists.*"* *The Washington Lawyer* (September/October 1995): 37ff.

———. *The Reporter and the Law: Techniques of Covering the Courts.* 2nd ed. New York: Columbia University Press, 1992, 1996.

Dershowitz, Alan. *Supreme Injustice: How the High Court Hijacked Election 2000.* New York: Oxford Press, 2001.

Deutsch, Linda. "Flash and Trash." *Media Studies Journal: Covering the Courts* 12:1 (Winter 1998): 50–53.

———. Foreword in Theo Wilson, *Headline Justice: Inside the Courtroom—The Country's Most Controversial Trials.* New York: Thunder's Mouth Press, 1996.

Deutsch, Linda, and Michael Fleeman. *Verdict: The Chronicle of the OJ Simpson Trial.* Kansas City, Mo.: Associated Press, 1995.

Dubos, Clancy. "That Phone Call from Hell: Facing the News Media on Behalf of a Client." *New Orleans Bar Association Briefly Speaking* (Fall 1993): 22.

Evarts, Dru Riley. "A Survey of the US Supreme Court Press Corps." Manuscript, Association for Education in Journalism and Mass Communication National Conference, Baltimore, 8 August 1998.

Fairchild, Ken. "Case-by-Case: Considering Media Impact.*"* *Texas Bar Journal* 58:5 (May 1995): 476–477.

Fanning, Rebecca. "The Court Officer: Meet the Press." *Media Studies Journal: Crime Story* 6:1 (Winter 1992): 94–103.

"Feds Release Transcript of Immigration Hearings." Reporters Committee for Freedom of the Press *The News Media and the Law* (Spring 2002): 47.

"The First Annual Symposium on Media and the Law: Free Speech v Fair Trial." *South Dakota Law Review* 41 (1996): 79–130.

Fitzpatrick, Kathy. "Free Speech v Fair Trial: A 50-State Analysis of Trial Publicity Rules." Manuscript, Association for Education in Journalism and Mass Communication National Convention, Baltimore, 8 August 1998.

The Florida Bar Association. *Reporter's Handbook.* Tallahassee: The Florida Bar Association, 1991.

France, Steve. "Supreme Court Report: A Penchant for Privacy." *ABA Journal* (December 1998): 38.

"From the Hotline." Reporters Committee for Freedom of the Press *The News Media and the Law* (Winter 2001): 28.

Garcia, Alfredo. "Clash of the Titans: The Difficult Reconciliation of a Free Trial and a Free Press in Modern American Society." *Santa Clara Law Review* 32 (1992): 1107–1133.

Gauthier, Ashley. "Secret Settlements: Hiding Defects, Hurting the Public." Reporters Committee for Freedom of the Press *The News Media and the Law* (Fall 2000): 3–7.

Gibson, Dirk, and Mariposa Podilla. "Litigation Public Relations Problems and Limits." *Public Relations Review* 28:2 (Summer 1999): 215–223.

Gold, Stuart. "Litigators and the Press." *Litigation* (Winter 1987): 36–38ff.

Goldfarb, Ronald. *TV or Not TV: Television, Justice, and the Courts.* New York: New York University Press, 1998.

Graham, Fred. "Doing Justice with Cameras in the Courts." *Media Studies Journal: Covering the Courts* 12:1 (Winter 1998): 32–37.

———. *Happy Talk: Confessions of a TV Newsman.* New York: W. W. Norton, 1990.

Gray, Cynthia. *Communicating with Voters: Ethics and Judicial Campaign Speech.* Chicago: American Judicature Society, 2000.

Harris, David. "The Appearance of Justice: Court TV, Conventional Television, and Public Understanding of the Criminal Justice System." *Arizona Law Review* 35 (1993): 785–827.

Hayslett, Jerrianne. *Tips for a Successful Media Plan on High Profile Trials.* Los Angeles: Administratively Unified Courts of Los Angeles County, 1993.

Higgins, Michael. "Rules to Talk by: Law Profs Propose an Ethics Code for Lawyer Commentators." American Bar Association *ABA Journal* (February 1998): 20–21.

Hodson, Thomas. "The Judge: Justice in Prime Time." *Media Studies Journal: Crime Story* 6:1 (Winter 1992): 86–93.

Howard, Roscoe. "The Media, Attorneys, and Fair Criminal Trials." *The Kansas Journal of Law and Public Policy* (Spring 1995): 61–75.

Johnson, Molly Treadway. "Electronic Media Coverage of Federal Civil Proceedings: An Evaluation of the Pilot Program in Six District Courts and Two Courts of Appeals." Manuscript, Federal Judicial Center Report to the Committee on Court Administration and Case Management of the Judicial Conference of the United States, November 1993.

———. "Electronic Media Coverage of Courtroom Proceedings: Effects on Witnesses and Jurors." Manuscript, Supplemental Report of the Federal Judicial Center to the Judicial Conference Committee on Court Administration and Case Management, 18 January 1994.

Judicial Conference Committee on Court Administration and Case Management. Report on Privacy and Public Access to Electronic Case Files, 26 June 2001.

"Judge Apologizes for Closed Proceeding." (Associated Press) *Washington Post*, 21 March 2000.

"Judge Modifies Gag Order in Ga Crematorium Case." Reporters Committee for Freedom of the Press *The News Media and the Law* (Spring 2002): 16.

"Judges Decide to Release Financial Disclosure Forms to News Service." Reporters Committee for Freedom of the Press *The News Media and the Law* (Spring 2000): 7–8.

"Judges to Allow Access to Some Criminal Cases." Reporters Committee for Freedom of the Press, www.rcfp.org (accessed June 2002).

Kamisar, Yale, Wayne LaFave, and Jerold Israel. *Modern Criminal Procedure: Cases, Comments, Questions.* 6th ed. St. Paul, Minn.: West Publishing, 1986.

Kaye, Hon. Judith. "The Third Branch and the Fourth Estate." *Media Studies Journal: Covering the Courts* 12:1 (Winter 1998): 74–79.

Keeva, Steve. "Storm Warnings." American Bar Association *ABA Journal* (June 1995): 77–78.

Kennedy, Randall. "Cast a Cautious Eye on the Supreme Court." *Media Studies Journal: Covering the Courts* 12:1 (Winter 1998): 112–123.

Kielbowicz, Richard. "The Story behind the Adoption of the Ban on Courtroom Cameras." *Judicature* 63:1 (June–July 1979): 14–23.

Killenberg, George. "Into the Legal Maze; The Trial and Thereafter," 205–262. In *Public Affairs Reporting: Covering the News in the Information Age*. New York: St. Martin's Press, 1992.

Krantz, Dick. "Covering the Courts." In *The Reporter's Handbook: An Investigator's Guide to Documents and Techniques*, 359–393, edited by John Ullmann and Steve Honeyman (IRE). New York: St. Martin's Press, 1983.

Lederer, Fredric. *The Road to the Virtual Courtroom? A Consideration of Today's—and Tomorrow's—High Technology Courtrooms*. Williamsburg, Va.: State Justice Institute/ William and Mary Law School, 1999.

Levin, Peter. "You Want Me to Read a What?" *Media Studies Journal: Crime Story* 6:1 (Winter 1992): 173–181.

"Litigation Public Relations: What to Do when Your Case Is Front Page News." (Panel Discussion, Annual Symposium, 24 February 1995). *The Review of Litigation* 14 (1995): 595–618.

Lovell, Ronald. "Courts." In *Reporting Public Affairs: Problems and Solutions*, 219–272. Prospect Heights, Ill.: Waveland Press, 1993.

Lukaszewski, James. "Managing Litigation Visibility: How to Avoid Lousy Trial Publicity." Public Relations Quarterly (Spring 1995): 28–24.

Mauro, Tony. "The Camera Shy Federal Courts." *Media Studies Journal: Covering the Courts* 12:1 (Winter 1998): 60–65.

———. Cited by Eveyln Theriot in *University of Southwest Louisiana: Society of Professional Journalists Verite* (Autumn 1996): 12.

McCullum, Edward. "The Advocate and the Media: The Courthouse Basement." 42 *Mercer Law Review* (1991): 875–882.

"Media Allowed to Attend Arraignment of Kennedy Nephew." (Associated Press) *Washington Post*, 10 March 2000.

Mencken, H. L., cited by Lloyd Chiasson, editor. *The Press on Trial: Crimes and Trials as Media Events*. Westport, Conn.: Greenwood Press, 1997.

Merritt, Hon. Gilbert S. "Justice by the Consent of the Governed: Interview With Judge Richard S. Arnold and Judge Gilbert S. Merritt." In *Media Studies Journal: Covering the Courts* 12:1 (Winter 1998): 80–91.

Moran, Tom. "Rules and Commandments for Dealing with the Press." *Texas Bar Journal* 58:5 (May 1995): 471–473.

Moreland, Mark. "Defending the High-Profile Client." *Trial* (April 1992): 24–31.

Moses, Jonathan. "Legal Spin Control: Ethics and Advocacy in the Court of Public Opinion." *Columbia Law Review* 95 (1995): 1811–1856.

Murphy, Timothy. *A Manual for Managing Notorious Trials*. Williamsburg, Va.: National Center for State Courts, 1992, 1998.

National Center for State Courts. "Summary of Television in the State Courts." Manuscript, NCSC, 2001.

National Judicial College. "Media and the Courts." Manuscript, NJC National Conference, 1996.

————. "Courts and Media—Conflict and Cooperation." Manuscript, NJC National Conference, 2000.

"New Jersey Judge Orders Release of 911 Tapes." Reporters Committee for Freedom of the Press, www.rcfp.org (accessed April 2002).

New Jersey Reporter's Handbook on Press Law and the Courts. Trenton: New Jersey Press Association/New Jersey State Bar Foundation, 1990.

Perez-Pena, Richard. "New York to Allow Bigger Fines on Lawyers' Nuisance Tactics." *New York Times*, 18 September 1997, sec. B6.

Petrocelli, Daniel, with Peter Knobler. *Triumph of Justice: The Final Judgment on the OJ Simpson Saga.* New York: Crown Publishers, 1998.

Possley, Maurice, and Rick Kogan. *Everybody Pays: Two Men, One Murder, and the Price of Truth.* New York: Putnam's Sons, 2001.

Pickerell, Albert, ed. *The Courts and the News Media.* San Francisco: California Judges Association, 1984.

Pollock, Donald. "Issues in Sensational or Widely Publicized Cases." Manuscript, Administrative Office of the Courts Legal Division, Miami, Florida, 1990.

"Proposed Policy on Court Records Threatens Public Access Rights." Reporters Committee for Freedom of the Press *The News Media and the Law* (Spring 2002): 8–9.

Radio-Television News Directors Association. "News Media Coverage of Judicial Proceedings with Cameras and Microphones: A Survey of the States." Manuscript, RTNDA, 2001.

Ramsey, Gail, and Kristen McGuire. "Litigation Publicity: Court Drama or Headline News." *Communications and the Law* (September 2000): 69–81.

Ray, Don. *Checking Out Lawyers.* (Spartenburg, S.C.: Military Information Enterprises, 1997).

Reporters Committee for Freedom of the Press. *Access to Juvenile Courts: A Reporter's Guide to Proceedings and Documents.* Washington, DC (periodic).

————. *The First Amendment Handbook* (periodic).

————. *Judicial Records: A Guide to Access in State and Federal Courts* (periodic).

————. *Secret Justice I: Anonymous Juries* (Fall 2000).

————. *Secret Justice II: Gag Orders* (Spring 2001).

————. *Secret Justice III: Alternative Dispute Resolution* (Fall 2001).

"Reporting on the Courts and the Law: A Workshop for Practicing Journalists." Manuscript, The Florida Bar Association/American Judicature Society, September 1990.

"Reporting the Law: Perspectives From the Press." Panel Discussion, Judicial Conference Second Circuit. *Federal Rules and Decisions* 160 (18 June 1994): 406–423.

Riccardi, Michael. "Lawyers, Press Examine Each Profession's Values: Media Attention Can Create Minefield in High-Profile Cases." *The Legal Intelligencer* 26 (September 1995): 1.

Roschwalb, Suzanne, and Richard Stack. *Litigation Public Relations: Courting Public Opinion.* Littleton, Colo.: Rothman and Co., 1995.

Roy, Mary-Ellen. "First Amendment Protects the Openness of Civil Trials." Investigative Reporters and Editors *IRE Journal* (March–April 2000): 11–13.

Sager, Kelli. "First Amendment Issues in the OJ Simpson Trial." *Communications Lawyer* (Winter 1995): 3–7.

Schmidt, Robert. "May It Please the Court." *Brill's Content* (October 1999): 73.

Schwartz, Bernard. *Decision: How the Supreme Court Decides Cases*. New York: Oxford University Press, 1996.

"Shall We Dance? The Courts, the Community and the News Media." *Judicature* 80:1 (July–August 1996): 30–42.

Shapiro, Robert. "Secrets of a Celebrity Lawyer." *Columbia Journalism Review* (September/October 1994): 25–29. Reprint of "Using the Media to Your Advantage" in *National Association of Criminal Defense Lawyers: The Champion* (January–February 1993).

Sharkey, Jacqueline. "Judgment Calls: The Media's OJ Obsession." *American Journalism Review* (September 1994): 18–27.

Sharp, Deborah. "Web-Wired Courtroom Lets World Attend Fla Trial." *USA Today*, 17 August 1999, sec. 3A.

Slotnick, Eliot, and Jennifer Segal. *Television News and the Supreme Court: All the News That's Fit to Air?* New York: Cambridge University Press, 1998.

Spencer, Gary. "Tougher Lawyer Sanction Rule Imposed: Clients' Rights Statement, Civility Code Also Issued." *New York Law Journal*, 18 September 1997, 1.

Stephen, Robert. "Prejudicial Publicity Surrounding a Criminal Trial: What a Trial Court Can Do to Ensure a Fair Trial in the Face of a 'Media Circus.'" *Suffolk University Law Review* 26 (1992): 1063–1106.

"Summary of the Report of the Judicial Conference Committee on Cameras in the Courtroom." Manuscript, Washington, DC, September 1990.

"Television Coverage of State Criminal Trials: Hon. CJ Gerald Kogan, Hon. Stanley Weisberg, Rikki Klieman." *St. Thomas Law Review* 9 (1997): 505–516.

Thaler, Paul. *The Spectacle: Media and the Making of the OJ Simpson Story*. Westport, Conn.: Praeger, 1997.

Tulsky, Fredric. "Courts." In *The Reporter's Handbook: An Investigator's Guide to Documents and Techniques*, 315–346, edited by John Ullmann and Jan Colbert (IRE). 2nd ed. New York: St. Martin's Press, 1991.

US Supreme Court Public Information Office. A Reporter's Guide to Applications Pending Before the Supreme Court of the US, at US Supreme Court, www.supremecourt.gov (accessed June 2002).

Waters, Robert. "Technology Can Remove Barriers to Free Information." *University of Florida Brechner Report* (February 1998): 4.

Watson, John. "Litigation Public Relations: Lawyers' Duty to Balance News Coverage of Their Clients." *Communications Law and Policy* 7:51 (2000): 77–103.

Weinberg, Steve. "Investigating Government: The Judicial System." In *The Reporter's Handbook: An Investigator's Guide to Documents and Techniques*, 217–269, edited by John Ullmann and Jan Colbert (IRE). 3rd ed. New York: St. Martin's Press, 1996.

Westfeldt, Wallace, and Tom Wicker. *Indictment: The News Media and the Criminal Justice System* (Nashville, Tenn.: First Amendment Center, 1998).

White, Frank. "Cameras in the Courtroom: A US Survey." *Journalism Monographs* 60 (April 1979).

Wieder, Robert. "How to Manipulate the Media: Twenty Timeless Tips for When the Press Comes Calling." *California Lawyer* (February 1994) 60–66.

Wilson, Duff. "Covering Courts: Off the Case." Manuscript, Investigative Reporters and Editors National Conference, New Orleans, 5 June 1998.

Zobel, Hon. Hiller. "Judicial Independence and the Need to Please." *The Judges Journal* (Fall 2001): 5–10.

LEGAL CITATIONS

Canon 3A(7). *Lawyers Manual on Professional Conduct*. (Chicago: American Bar Association, 1982).

Canon 35. *American Bar Association Reports* 62 (1937): 1134–1135.

Federal Rules of Civil Procedure.

Federal Rules of Criminal Procedure.

Federal Rules of Evidence for Judges and Magistrates.

Fla Stat Sect 406.135 Public Health, Medical Examiners: Autopsies; confidentiality of photographs and video and audio recordings, 2001.

La R S 44:19 Public Records and Recorders: Autopsy photographs, video, and other visual images, 2002.

Model Policy on Public Access to Court Records, at www.ncsconline.org, 2002.

Sunshine in the Courtroom Act, 105th Congress, 1st Session HR 1280, 1997; *Judicial Reform Act*, 2000, HR 1252; *A Bill to Allow Media Coverage of Court Proceedings*, 107th Cong, S 986, HR 2519, 2001.

The Terrorist Victims' Courtroom Access Act. 107th Cong, 2nd Sess, 2002 S 1858, 107S 1858.

US v Clinton, US GPO S doc 106th Cong, 1st Sess, 1999, Sen 106–104.

Uniform Mediation Act, National Conference of Commissioners on Uniform State Laws, at www.nccusl.org, 2001.

CASES

Albuquerque Journal v Jewell, 130 NM 64 (NM Sup Ct), 2001.

Anonymous v Anonymous, 263 AD 2d 341 (NY Sup Ct Appl), 2000.

Arkansas Democrat-Gazette v Zimmerman, 341 Ark 771 (Ark Sup Ct), 2000.

Ashcraft v Conoco, 218 F 3d 282, 218 F 3d 288 (US Ct Appl 4th Cir), 2000.

Batson v Kentucky, 476 US 79, 1986.

Branzburg v Hayes, 408 US 665, 1972.

Broadman v Commission on Judicial Performance, 18 Cal 4th 1079 (Ca Sup Ct), 1998.

Bush v Gore, 531 US 98, 2000.

California v Menendez, Ca Super Court L A Cty SC 031947, 1995; Ca Super Ct LA Cty SA 002727, SA 002728, 1994.

In re California v Simpson, No BAO 97211 (Proceedings 11/7/94).

Cape Publications v Braden, 39 SW 3d 823 (KY Sup Ct), 2001.

Chandler v Florida, 449 US 560, 1981.

Chicago Tribune v Bridgestone/Firestone, 263 F 3d 1304 (US 11th Cir Ct Appl), 2001.

Commonwealth v Gallman, 48 Pa D & C 4th 413 (Phil Ct Comm Pleas) 2001.

Commonwealth v Woodward, Supr Ct Mass Middlesex 97–0433, 1997; *affm'd* 427 Mass 659, 1998.

Cox Broadcasting v Cohn, 420 US 469, 1975.

Craig v Harney, 331 US 367, 1947.

Daily News v Teresi, 265 AD 2d 129 (Sup Ct of NY Appl Div), 2000.

In re Daily Journal v Police Dept of Vineland, 797 A 2d 186 (Supr Ct NJ) 2001.

Devine v Robinson, 131 F Supp 2d 963 (US Dist Ct N Dist IL), 2001.

In re Domestic Air Transportation Antitrust Litigation, 24 Fed R Serv 3d (Callaghan) 515 (US Dist Ct MD Ga), 1994.

In re Dow Jones and Co Publications, US App (DC Cir) 27 Med. L Rptr 1156, 1997.

Dow Jones v Kaye, 256 F 3d 1251 (US 11th Cir Ct Appl) 2001.

Earnhardt v Volusia Cty, Fla Cir Ct Volusia Cty, 29 Med L Rptr 2173, 2001.

El Vocero de Puerto Rico v Puerto Rico, 508 US 147, 1993.

Entertain v Lappin, 134 F Supp 2d 1002 (US Dist Ct, SD Ind), 2001.

Estes v Texas, 381 US 532, 1965.

Federated v. Swedburg, 633 P2d 74 (Wash Sup Ct), 1981; *cert den* 456 US 984, 1982.

Florida Bar v Went For It, 515 US 618, 1995.

Florida Star v BJF, 491 US 524, 1989.

Gannett v DePasquale, 443 US 368. 1979.

Gentile v State Bar of Nevada, 501 US 1030, 1991.

Globe Newspaper v Sup Ct, 457 US 596, 1982.

In re Houston Chronicle, 64 SW 3d 103 (Tex Ct Appl, 14th Dist), 2001.

Irvin v. Dowd, 366 US 717, 1961.

JEB v Alabama, 511 US 127, 1994.

Jeffries v Mississippi, 724 So 2d 897 (Miss Sup Ct), 1998.

Jessup v Luther, 277 F 3d 926 (US 7th Cir Ct Appl), 2002.

Jones v Clinton, US Dist Ct ED Ark No LR-C-94–290, 27 Med. L Rptr 1156, 1998.

Landmark Communications v Virginia, 435 US 829, 1978.

Leggett v US, In re Grand Jury Subpoenas, US Ct Appl 5th Cir (unpublished opinion), No 01–20745, 29 Med L Rptr 2301, 2001; *cert den* 122 S Ct 1593, 2002.

McNaghten's (M'Naghten's) Case, 8 Eng Rep 718 (1843).

In re Memphis Publishing, 29 Med L Rptr 2565 (Miss Sup Ct), 2001.

Miranda v Arizona, 384 US 436, 1966.

Mu'Min v Virginia, 501 US 1269, 1991.

In re NBC, 648 F2d 814 (US 3rd Cir Ct Appl), 1981.

NBC (KNBC) v Supr Ct L A, 20 Cal 4th 1178 (CA Sup Ct), 1999.

Nebraska Press Association v Stuart, 427 US 539, 1976.

New Jersey v Hauptmann, 180 A 809 (NJ Sup Ct), 1935; *cert den* 296 US 649 (1935).

New Jersey v Neulander, 171 NJ 332 (unpublished opinion), 2002.

New York v Boss, 261 AD 211 (NY Sup Ct Albany Cty), 2000.

Nichols v Dist Ct Oklahoma Cty, 2000 OK CR 12, PR 2000–703 (OK Ct Criminal Appls), 2000.

Nixon v. Warner Communications, 435 US 589, 1978.

Ohio ex rel Dispatch Printing v Louden, 741 NE 2d 517 (Ohio Sup Ct), 2001.

Oregonian Publishing v US Dist Ct, 920 F 2d 1462 (US 9th Cir Ct Appl), 1990.

Phoenix News v US Dist Ct, 156 F 3d 940 (US 9th Cir Ct Appl), 1998.

Pittman v Cole, 267 F 3d 1269 (US 11th Cir Ct Appl), 2001.

Press Enterprise v Riverside Sup Ct I, 464 US 501, 1984.

Press Enterprise v Riverside Sup Ct II, 478 US 1, 1986.
In re Providence Journal, 820 F2d 1342 (US 1st Cir Ct Appl), 1986; *mod.* 820 F2d 1354 (US 1st Cir Ct Appl), 1987; *cert den* 485 US 693, 1988.
Republican Party of Minnesota v White, 122 S Ct 2528, 2002.
In re Request for Transcripts, 26 Med L Rptr 2073 (Ca 4th Dist Ct Appl), 1998.
Richmond Newspapers v Virginia, 448 US 555, 1980.
Rideau v. Louisiana, 373 US 723, 1963.
In re Rufo v Simpson, Ca Sup Ct No SC 031947 (23 August 1996).
Seattle Times v Rhinehart, 467 US 20, 1984.
Sheppard v Maxwell, Warden, 384 US 333, 1966.
In re Siegel v LePore, 29 Med L Rptr 1190 (US Dist Ct, SD Fla), 2000.
Smith v Daily Mail, 443 US 97, 1979.
Smith v Richmond News, 261 Va 113 (Va Sup Ct), 2001.
Unabomb Trial Media Coalition v US Dist Ct ED CA, 183 F 3d 949, (US 9th Cir Ct Appl), 1999.
US v Brown, 25 F 3d 907 (US 5th Cir Ct Appl), 2001; 218 F 3d 415 (US Ct Appl 5th Cir), 2000.
US v Burr, 25 Fed Cas 49 No 14692g (1807).
In re US v Cleveland, 128 F 3d 267 (US 5th Cir Ct Appl, 1997); *cert den, In re Capital City Press*, 523 US 1075, 1998.
US v Dickinson, 465 F2d 496 (US 5th Cir Ct Appl), 1972.
US v Edwards, US 5th Cir Ct Appl, MD La, 98–165-B M2, 2000; 119 F Supp 2d 589 (US 5th Cir Ct Appl), 2000.
US v Jackson, 969 F Supp 881 (SD NY), 1997.
In re US v King, 140 F 3d 76 (US Ct Appl DC Cir), 1998.
US v Ladd, 218 F 3d 701 (US 7th Cir Ct Appl), 2000.
US v McVeigh and Nichols, 153 F 3d 1166 (US 10th Cir Ct Appl), 1998; 169 F 3d 1255 (US 10th Cir Ct Appl, 1997); 955 F Supp 1281 (US Dist Ct, Dist CO), 1997; 931 F Supp 753 (US Dist Ct, Dist CO), 1996; 918 F Supp 1467 (US Dist Ct, Dist CO), 1996; *In re Petition of Colorado-Oklahoma Media*, 964 F Supp 313 (US Dist Ct, Dist CO), 1997; 119 F 3d 806 (US 10th Cir Ct Appl), 1997.
In re US v Noriega, 752 F Supp 1032 (US Dist Ct DC), 1990; 917 F 2d 1543 (US 11th Cir Ct Appl), 1990; *cert den, Cable News Network v Noriega and US*, 498 US 976, 1990.
US v Microsoft, 253 F 3d 34, 2001;US Dist Ct DC 98–1232, 98–1233, 2000; 334 US App DC 165, 1999;
US v Moussaoui, US Dist Ct ED Va, No 01–455-A, 2002.
US v Scarfo, 263 F 3d 80 (US 3rd Cir Ct Appl), 2001.
US v Smith, 992 F Supp 743 (US Dist Ct NJ), 1998.
Waller v Georgia, 467 US 39, 1984.

INTERVIEWS

Angelico, Richard. New Orleans, 20 November; 3 December 1997.
Bosco, Joseph. (telephone) 22 August 1996; New Orleans, 24 November 1997.

Bragg, Rick. New Orleans, 3 July 2002.

Burton, Eve, Esq. New Orleans, 5 June 1998.

Bransetter, Ziva. Lafayette, Louisiana, 30 March 1996.

Coyle, Pamela. New Orleans, 5 March 1998.

Dershowitz, Alan, Esq. New Orleans, 3 June 2002; (telephone) 16 July 2002.

Deutsch, Linda. Los Angeles, August 1996; (telephone) 22 August 1996; New Orleans, 6 October 1997.

French, Thomas. Columbus, Ohio, 20 October 2000.

Gest, Ted. Reno, 9 June 2000; (telephone) 2 July 2002.

Gauthier, Wendell, Esq. New Orleans, 15 October 1997. (Deceased 2001)

Graham, Fred, Esq. New Orleans, 27 October 1997.

Greenhouse, Linda, New Orleans, 24 October 2000.

Leval, Pierre, Hon. New Orleans, 14 April 1998.

Lithwick, Dahlia, Esq. Reno, 9 June 2000; (telephone) 22 June 2000.

Mauro, Tony. Reno, 9 June 2000; (telephone) 5 July 2002.

Mintz, Howard. Baton Rouge, Louisiana, 29 March 2000.

O'Brien, Tim, Esq. New Orleans, May 1997; (telephone) 19 May 1997.

Okrasinski, Jane, Esq. New Orleans, 22 May 1996.

Possley, Maurice. Baton Rouge, Louisiana, 29 March 2000.

Ray, Don. New Orleans, 5 June 1998.

Stockton, Ethel. Ocala, Florida, 31 July 1989.

Talley, Tim. Lafayette, Louisiana, 30 March 1996.

Totenberg, Nina. (telephone) 16 July 2002.

Varney, James. New Orleans, 17 September 1997.

Wilson, Duff. New Orleans, 5 June 1999.

Zobel, Hon. Hiller. Reno, 9 June 2000; (telephone) 22 July 2002.

WEBSITES

Administrative Office of the US Courts, www.uscourts.gov

American Bar Association, www.abanet.org

American Bar Association Journal, www.abajournal.com

American Board of Trial Advocates, www.abota.org

American Lawyer, www.americanlawyer.com

Bureau of Justice Statistics, www.ojp.usdoj.gov

Cornell University Law School, www.supct.law.cornell.edu

Court TV, www.courttv.com

Criminal Justice Journalists, www.reporters.net/cjj

Emory University School of Law, "Emory Law School Federal Courts Finder," www. law.emory.edu/FEDCTS

Federal Judicial Center, www.fjc.gov

Find Law, www.findlaw.com

Investigative Reporters and Editors, www.ire.org

Law.Com, www.law.com

Lawyers Weekly, www.lawyersweekly.com

Legal Times, www.legaltimes.com (via www.law.com)

Lexis One, www.lexisone.com

Martindale Hubbell, www.martindale.com

National Archives Records Administration, www.gpo.gov/nara/index.

National Association of Attorneys General, www.naag.org

National Association of Criminal Defense Lawyers, www.nacdl.org

National Association of State Sentencing Commissions, www.ussc.gov/states

National Center for State Courts, www.ncsonline.org

National District Attorneys Association, www.ndaa.org

National Judicial College Center for the Courts and Media, www.judges.org

National Law Journal, www.nlj.com

New York Times, www.nyt.com

Northwestern University Law School, "On the Docket," www.medill.northwestern.edu/docket

Public Access to Courts Electronic Records (PACER), www.pacer.psc.uscourts.gov

Radio-Television News Directors' Association, www.rtnda.org

Reporters Committee for Freedom of the Press, www.rcfp.org

Society of Professional Journalists, www.spj.org

Stanford University Law School, "Security Class Action Clearinghouse," www.securities.stanford.edu

US Department of Justice, www.ojp.usdoj.gov

US Sentencing Commission, www.ussc.gov

US Supreme Court, www.supremecourt.gov

West Doc, www.westdoc.com

West Legal Directory, www.directory.findlaw.com

Index

Italicized numbers indicate references to figures

About the Author

S. L. Alexander, Ph.D., is a journalist and coordinator of communications law on the communications faculty at Loyola University in New Orleans. She has worked in print and broadcast news and earned her Ph.D. in communications law at the University of Florida in 1990 with a study of courtroom coverage. She is active in various press organizations including the Society of Professional Journalists, and has written extensively on press coverage of courts, including the upcoming reference work *Media and American Courts* (ABC-CLIO, 2003). She is currently working on a collection, *Courtroom Carnival: Tales of New Orleans Courtrooms.*